SPOTLIGHT on MUSIC ™

Authors

Judy Bond

René Boyer

Margaret Campbelle-Holman

Emily Crocker

Marilyn C. Davidson

Robert de Frece

Virginia Ebinger

Mary Goetze

Betsy M. Henderson

John Jacobson

Michael Jothen

Chris Judah-Lauder

Carol King

Vincent P. Lawrence

Ellen McCullough-Brabson

Janet McMillion

Nancy L. T. Miller

Ivy Rawlins

Susan Snyder

Gilberto D. Soto

Kodály Contributing Consultant

Sr. Lorna Zemke

McGraw Hill

HAL•LEONARD®

MACMILLAN McGRAW-HILL

ACKNOWLEDGMENTS

Creative Direction and Delivery: The Quarasan Group, Inc.

From the Top-On National Radio! selections are adapted from the nationally distributed public radio program, *From the Top.* CEOs/Executive Producers: Jennifer Hurley-Wales and Gerald Slavet. Authors: Ann Gregg and Joanne Robinson. © 2000, 2002, 2003 From the Top, Inc.

The Broadway Junior® logo and MTI® logo are trademarks of Music Theatre International. All rights reserved.

Grateful acknowledgment is given to the following authors, composers, and publishers. Every effort has been made to trace the ownership of all copyrighted material and to secure the necessary permissions to reprint these selections. In the case of some selections for which acknowledgment is not given, extensive research has failed to locate the copyright holders.

Songs and Speech Pieces

Apple Picker's Reel, Words and Music by Larry Hanks. Copyright © 1967. Alpha Film Music. International Copyright Secured. All Rights Reserved.

Artichokes, Words and Music by Malvina Reynolds. Copyright © Schroder Music Company. International Copyright Secured. All Rights Reserved.

Baby Beluga, Words and Music by Raffi Cavoukian and D. Pike. Copyright © 1980 by Homeland Publishing, a div. of Troubadour Music, Inc. International Copyright Secured. All Rights Reserved.

Ban Dal (Half Moon), Words and Music by Keuk Young Youn. Copyright © by SEH KWANG PUBLISHING CO. International Copyright Secured. All Rights Reserved.

Bate, bate, Adapted by José-Luis Orozco. Copyright © 1989 by Arcoiris Records, Inc. International Copyright Secured. All Rights Reserved.

Big Beautiful Planet, Words and Music by Raffi Cavoukian. Copyright © by Homeland Publishing, a div. of Troubadour Music, Inc. International Copyright Secured. All Rights Reserved.

Candle on the Water, from *Walt Disney's PETE'S DRAGON.* Words and Music by Al Kasha and Joel Hirschhorn. Copyright © 1976 Walt Disney Music Company and Wonderland Music Company, Inc. All Rights Reserved. Used by Permission.

Check It Out! (It's About Respect), Words and Music by John Jacobson and John Higgins. Copyright © 2001 by MUSIC EXPRESS LLC. International Copyright Secured. All Rights Reserved.

Columbus Sailed with Three Ships, Words and Music by Margaret Campbelle-Holman. Copyright © 1981 by Margaret Campbelle-Holman. International Copyright Secured. All Rights Reserved.

Dal taro kacha (Come, Pick the Moon), Words by Suk-Joong Yoon. Music by Tae-Hyun Park, Copyright © by SEH KWANG PUBLISHING CO. International Copyright Secured. All Rights Reserved.

Dance, Dance, Dance!, Words by Ava Hogan Chapman. Music by Moses Hogan. Copyright © 2001 by MUSIC EXPRESS LLC. International Copyright Secured. All Rights Reserved.

Do-Re-Mi, *from THE SOUND OF MUSIC®.* Lyrics by Oscar Hammerstein II. Music by Richard Rodgers. Copyright © 1959 by Richard Rodgers and Oscar Hammerstein II. Copyright Renewed. WILLIAMSON MUSIC owner of publication and allied rights throughout the world International Copyright Secured. All Rights Reserved. The Sound Of Music is a registered trademark used under license from The Rodgers and Hammerstein Organization on behalf of the Rodgers Family Partnership, the Estate of Oscar Hammerstein II and the heirs of Howard Lindsay and Russel Crouse.

Eating Lizards, Words and Music by Carol Huffman.

El burrito enfermo (The Sick Little Donkey), Latin American Folk Song. Adapted by José-Luis Orozco. Copyright © by José-Luis Orozco/Arcoiris Records, P.O. Box 461900, Los Angeles, CA 90046. International Copyright Secured. All Rights Reserved.

En nuestra Tierra tan linda (On Our Beautiful Planet Earth), Latin American Folk Song. Adapted by José-Luis Orozco. Copyright © 1996 by José-Luis Orozco/Arcoiris Records, P.O. Box 461900, Los Angeles, CA 90046. International Copyright Secured. All Rights Reserved.

El palomo y la paloma (The Doves), Mexican Folk Song. Adapted by José-Luis Orozco. Copyright © 1996 by José-Luis Orozco/Arcoiris Records, P.O. Box 461900, Los Angeles, CA 90046. International Copyright Secured. All Rights Reserved.

Everybody Has Music Inside, Words and Music by Greg Scelsa. Copyright © 1980 Little House Music (ASCAP). International Copyright Secured. All Rights Reserved.

Everything Grows, Words and Music by Raffi Cavoukian and D. Pike. Copyright © 1987 by Homeland Publishing, a div. of Troubadour Music, Inc. International Copyright Secured. All Rights Reserved.

Food Song, The, Words and Music by Jackie Silberg. Copyright © 1989 by Miss Jackie Music Company. International Copyright Secured. All Rights Reserved.

Garden Song, Words and Music by Dave Mallett. Copyright © 1975. Cherry Lane Music Publishing Company, Inc. (ASCAP) and DreamWorks Songs (ASCAP). Worldwide Rights for DreamWorks Songs Administered by Cherry Lane Music Publishing Company, Inc. International Copyright Secured. All Rights Reserved.

continued on page 393

The McGraw·Hill Companies

Published by Macmillan/McGraw-Hill, of McGraw-Hill Education, a division of The McGraw-Hill Companies, Inc., Two Penn Plaza, New York, New York 10121.

Printed in the United States of America
ISBN 0-02-295675-1 / 2
8 9 110/043 10 09 08 07 06

SPOTLIGHT on MUSIC

CONTRIBUTORS

Consultants

Brian Burnett,
Movement

Stephen Gabriel,
Technology

Magali Iglesias,
English Language Learners

Roberta Newcomer,
Special Learners/Assessment

Frank Rodríguez,
English Language Learners

Jacque Schrader,
Movement

Kathy B. Sorensen,
International Phonetic Alphabet

Patti Windes-Bridges,
Listening Maps

Linda Worsley,
Listening/Singable English Translations

Sr. Lorna Zemke,
Kodály Contributing Consultant

Contributing Writers

Allison Abucewicz
Sharon Berndt
Rhona Brink
Ann Burbridge
Debbie Helm Daniel
Katherine Domingo
Kari Gilbertson
Janet Graham
Hilree Hamilton
Linda Harley
Judy Henneberger
Carol Huffman
Bernie Hynson, Jr.
Sheila A. Kerley
Ellen Mendelsohn

Cristi Cary Miller
Leigh Ann Mock
Patricia O'Rourke
Barbara Resch
Isabel Romero
Carl B. Schmidt
Debra Shearer
Ellen Mundy Shuler
Rebecca Treadway
Carol Wheeler
Sheila Woodward

Recordings

Executive Producer
John Higgins

Senior Music Editor/Producer
Emily Crocker

Senior Recording Producer
Mark Brymer

Recording Producers
Steve Millikan
Andy Waterman

Associate Recording Producers
Alan Billingsley, Darrell Bledsoe, Stacy Carson, Emily Crocker, Rosanna

Eckert, John Egan, Chad Evans, Darlene Koldenhoven, Chris Koszuta, Don Markese, Matthew McGregor, Steve Potts, Edwin Schupman, Michael Spresser, Frank Stegall, David Vartanian, Mike Wilson, Ted Wilson

Project/Mastering Engineer
Mark Aspinall

Post Production Engineer
Don Sternecker

Multicultural Consultants

William Anderson, Chet-Yeng Loong, Edwin Schupman, Kathy B. Sorensen, Gilberto D. Soto, Judith Cook Tucker, Dennis Waring

In the Spotlight Consultant

Willa Dunleavy

Multicultural Advisors

Brad Ahawanrathe Bonaparte (Mohawk), Emmanuel Akakpo (Ewe), Earlene Albano (Hawaiian), Luana Au (Maori), Ruby Beeston (Mandarin), Latif Bolat (Turkey), Estella Christensen (Spanish), Oussama Davis (Arabic), Mia Delguardo (Minahasa), Nolutho Ndengane Diko (Xhosa), Angela Fields (Hopi, Chemehuevi), Gary Fields (Lakota, Cree), Gilad Harel (Hebrew), Josephine Hetarihon (Bahasa Indonesian, Minahasa, and Maluko dialect), Judy Hirt-Manheimer (Hebrew), Rose Jakub (Navajo), Elizabeth Jarema (Fijian), Rita Jensen (Swedish), Malou Jewett (Visayan), Alejandro Jimenez (Hispanic), Chris Jones (Hungarian), Wendy Jyang Shamo (Mandarin), Amir Kalay (Hebrew), Michael Katsan (Greek), Silvi Madarajan (Tamil), Georgia Magpie (Comanche), Nona Mardi (Malay), Aida Mattingly (Tagalog), Mike Kanathohare McDonald (Mohawk), Vasana de Mel (Sinhala), Marion Miller (Czech), Etsuko Miskin (Japanese), Mogens Mogenson (Danish), Kenny Tahawisoren Perkins (Mohawk), Pradeep Nayyar (Punjabi, Hindi), Renu Nayyar (Punjabi), Mfanego Ngwenya (Zulu), Wil Numkena (Hopi), Samuel Owuru (Akan), Nina Padukone (Konkani), Hung Yong Park (Korean), James Parker (Finnish), Jose Pereira (Konkani), Berrit Price (Norwegian), John Rainer (Taos Pueblo, Creek), Lillian Rainer (Taos Pueblo, Creek, Apache), Arnold Richardson (Haliwa-Saponi), Ken Runnacles (German), Trudy Shenk (German), Ron Singer (Navajo), Ernest Siva (Cahuilla, Serrano [Maringa']), Bonnie Slade (Swedish), Cristina Sorrentino (Portuguese), Diane Thram (Xhosa), Elena Todorov (Bulgarian), Zlatina Todorov (Russian), Tom Toronto (Lao, Thai), Rebecca Wilberg (French, Italian), Sheila Woodward (Zulu), Keith Yackeyonny (Comanche)

Contents

Spotlight on Celebrations.............337

In the Spotlight

There is a light that shines
bright in the All-American sky.
It sings! It plays!
It dances like the sun!
There is a light that shines in America!
I want to step into that light!

Step into the Spotlight

Spotlight CD
Track 1

Words and Music by John Jacobson,
Emily Crocker, and John Higgins

1. Lis - ten to the world a - round you, There is
2. In a world of sound and col - or, in a

mus - ic ev - 'ry - where.___ Just step out - side___ your
rhy - thm all its own,___ It's the heart - beat of___ A -

door - way, and you can hear mus - ic in the air!___
mer - i - ca, the land we proud - ly call our home!_

From the cit - y to the farm and field,___ to the
From the cit - y to the farm and field,___ there's a

A

But wait … where shall we start?
Let's start at the very beginning.
It's a very good place to start!

Do-Re-Mi

from the movie *The Sound of Music*

**Spotlight CD
Track 4**

Lyrics by Oscar Hammerstein II
Music by Richard Rodgers

Doe, a deer, a fe - male deer,

Ray, a drop of gold - en sun,

Me, a name I call my - self,

Far, a long, long way to run.

Sew, a nee - dle pull - ing thread,

La, a note to fol - low sew,

Tea, a drink with jam and bread,

1.
That will bring us back to do - oh - oh - oh!

2.
bring us back to doe!

Do - re - mi - fa - so - la - ti - do!

D

There is a light that shines in America.
Full of hope and pride.
I see it now!
The light that shines in America is me!

This Little Light of Mine

Spotlight CD
Track 7

Freely

African American Spiritual

This lit-tle light of mine, __ I'm gon-na let it shine. __

This lit-tle light of mine, __ I'm gon-na let it shine. __

This lit-tle light of mine, __ I'm gon-na let it shine. __

Let it shine, __ let it shine, __ let it shine. __

2. Down in my heart, I'm gonna let it shine.
   Down in my heart, I'm gonna let it shine.
   Down in my heart, I'm gonna let it shine.
   Let it shine, let it shine, let it shine.

3. All over the world, I'm gonna let it shine.
   All over the world, I'm gonna let it shine.
   All over the world, I'm gonna let it shine.
   Let it shine, let it shine, let it shine.

When I sing the songs of
America all by myself,
I show how much
I love my country.
When we sing our songs
of America together,
we make harmony!
Then the light that shines in
America burns brighter for all!

Patriotic Medley

Spotlight CD Track 10

Words by George M. Cohan
Woody Guthrie, and Katharine Lee Bates.

You're a Grand Old Flag

You're a Grand Old Flag, you're a high flyin' flag.
And forever in peace may you wave.
You're the emblem of the land I love,
The home of the free and the brave.
Ev'ry heart beats true
    for the red, white, and blue,
Where there's never a boast or brag.
But should auld acquaintance be forgot,
Keep your eye on the grand old flag.

This Land Is Your Land

This land is your land, this land is my land
From California to the New York Island.
From the redwood forest
    to the Gulf Stream waters,
This land was made for you and me.
As I was walking that ribbon of highway,
I saw above me that endless skyway.
I saw below me that golden valley.
This land was made for you and me.

America!

America! America! God shed His grace on thee.
And crown thy good with brotherhood,
From sea to shining sea! (*Repeat last two lines*)

Spotlight on
Concepts

Spotlight on Concepts

Spotlight on Concepts

Together Through Music

How are these children making music?

Coming Attractions

Move with the beat to a jump-rope rhyme.

Play along with ballet music.

Sing about lemonade on *so* and *mi*.

Music is one way we can
work and play together.

Sing and move together with the song.

CD 1:1

Music by Moses Hogan
Words by Ava Hogan-Chapman

A

Hop, hop, hop, Hop___ to your feet. Just jump, jump, jump,

Jump___ to the beat. Let's dance, dance, dance,

Danc - ing is fun for ev' - ry - one.

B

1. Wig-gle it, wig - gle it, Jump it, jump it,
(Gr. 1) 2. Swing_ it high,_____ *(Gr. 2) swing it low,____*

Hop it, *hop it,* Bop it, *bop it,* } Move it, *move it,* Groove it, *groove it,*
Swing it fast,_ *swing it slow,_*

(Second time to A *)*

'Til your bo - dy can't stop mov - in'.

5

Step to the Beat

CONCEPT
RHYTHM
SKILLS
SING, MOVE, LISTEN
LINKS
CULTURES

The steady pulse you feel in music is called **beat**. **Pat** with the beat as you learn this song. Then march to it!

Step In Time

from the movie *Mary Poppins*

CD 1:4

Words and Music by Richard M. Sherman and Robert B. Sherman

1. Kick your knees up, step in time!
2. Link your el - bows, step in time!
3. Spin a - bout and step in time!
4. 'Round the chim - ney, step in time!

Kick your knees up, step in time!
Link your el - bows, step in time!
Spin a - bout and step in time!
'Round the chim - ney, step in time!

Nev - er need a rea - son, nev - er need a rhyme,
Nev - er need a rea - son, nev - er need a rhyme,

Kick your knees up, step in time!
Link your el - bows, step in time!
Spin a - bout and step in time!
'Round the chim - ney, step in time!

6

5. Flap like a bird - ie, step in time!
6. Step in____ time,____ step in time!

Flap like a bird - ie, step in time!
Step in____ time,____ step in time!

Nev - er need a rea - son, nev - er need a rhyme,
Nev - er need a rea - son, nev - er need a rhyme, when you

1.
Flap like a bird - ie, step in time!

2.
step in time, you step in time.

Beat and Rhythm

When you jump rope, you jump with the beat.
Move to the beat and say this jump-rope rhyme.

Skipping rope started a long time ago. ▶
At first mostly boys played it. Now girls play it too.

Sheep in the Meadow

 CD 1:7

Sheep in the meadow,
Cows in the corn.
Jump in on the month
    that you were born.
January, February, March, April,
May, June, July, August,
September, October,
November, December!

The Boys Choir of Harlem

Pat with the beat as you **listen**.

 LISTENING CD 1:10

Little David, Play on Your Harp (African American Spiritual)

The long and short sounds in a song are
called **rhythm**. Clap the rhythm.

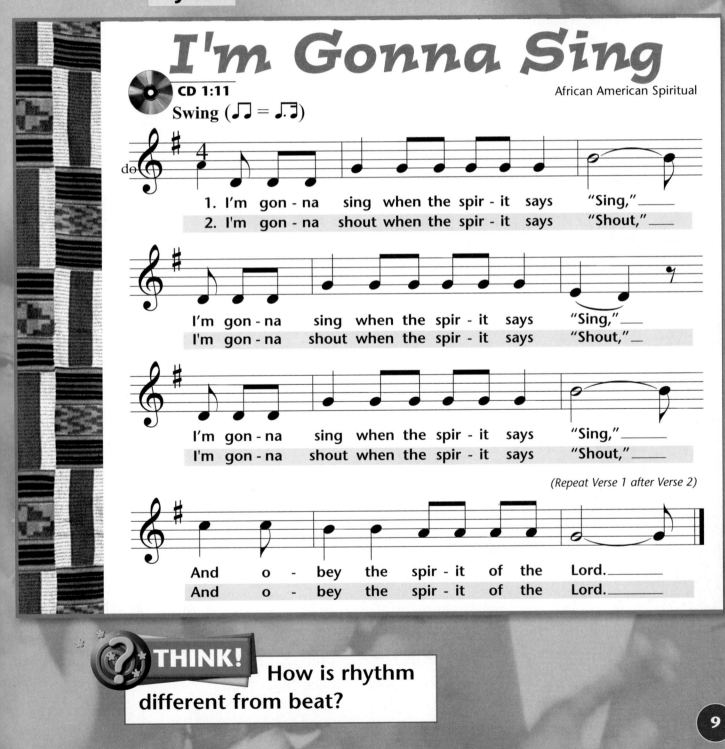

THINK! How is rhythm
different from beat?

CONCEPT
MELODY

SKILLS
SING, READ, MOVE

LINKS
SOCIAL STUDIES, FINE ART

Respect is an important part of being a good citizen. **Sing** this song about respect. Can you tell when the melody moves higher and when it moves lower?

Check It Out! (It's About Respect)

CD 1:14

Words and Music by
John Higgins and John Jacobson

It's a - bout re - spect! Check it out! Check it out!

(Repeat **A** after **B** and **C**)

It's a - bout re - spect! Check it out!

10

Ⓑ

Got - ta   treat   my friends like   fam - i - ly.___   Got - ta

treat   my fam - i - ly   like   friends.___   Treat 'em

with   re - spect   and they'll be there for   me.___   They can

count   on   me   in   the   end.___

Spoken:

C

R! There's a reason people treat you like they do.

E! Ev'rybody take a chance.

S! It's so simple, and it all begins with you.

P! People gotta take a stand.

E! Even when you think the world isn't fair.

C! Come along and check it out!

T! Take a risk, take a ride, take a dare.

Take a breath of air and let's shout, RESPECT!

Check it out! RESPECT! Check it out!

Higher and Lower Melody

Pitch is how high or low a sound is.
A group of pitches is a **melody**.

Listen to "Engine, Engine Number Nine."
How are the pictures below like the melody?

In music, pitches are shown with **notes** on
five lines called a **staff**.

staff

note

Sing this song. Move higher and lower with the melody.

ENGINE, ENGINE NUMBER NINE

CD 1:17

American Song

En-gine, en-gine, num-ber nine, go-ing down the rail-road line!

If the train goes off the track, will I get my mon-ey back?

Art Gallery

Train in Coal Town by Jack Savitsky

Jack Savitsky worked in the coal mines. He taught himself to draw and paint. He often drew on the walls of the tunnels in the coal mines.

CONCEPT
RHYTHM
SKILLS
READ, SING,
PLAY
LINKS
MATH, SCIENCE,
SOCIAL STUDIES

You can show one sound to a beat with a **quarter note**.

You can show two equal sounds to a beat with two **eighth notes**.

Music has beats of silence as well as sounds. **Listen** for beats of silence in this song.

🔘 **LISTENING** / CD 1:20

I Bought Me a Cat arranged by Aaron Copland

You can show a beat of silence with a **quarter rest**. Find the 𝄽 in the song.

I Bought Me a Cat

CD 1:21

Kentucky Mountain Folk Song

1. I bought me a cat, and the cat pleased me.

I fed my cat un - der yon - der tree.

Cat goes fid - dle - i - fee.

2.-5. I bought me a
hen, and the hen pleased me.
duck, and the duck pleased me.
goose, and the goose pleased me.
pig, and the pig pleased me.

I fed my
hen
duck
goose
pig
un - der yon - der tree.

(Cumulative: For each new verse, add lines above.)

Hen goes chim - my chuck, chim - my chuck.
Duck goes quack,____ quack.____
Goose goes honk,____ honk.____
Pig goes grif - fy, grif - fy.

Cat goes fid - dle - i - fee.

6. Cow: moo, moo
7. Horse: neigh, neigh

Read these rhythms. Match each animal sound with a rhythm.

a.

b.

c.

d.

Playing Rhythms

Look at the Playalong. What do you think the beat bars with no instruments show?

LISTENING CD 1:24

Country Gardens by Percy Grainger

Play rhythm instruments as you listen.

KEY

Tap your sticks together.

Tap your sticks lightly on the desk or on the floor.

Play the wood block.

Play the triangle.

Play the drum.

Playalong and Listening Map for *Country Gardens*

Meet the Musician

Percy Grainger was an Australian composer and pianist. He began playing concerts when he was ten years old. Grainger collected English folk songs. He used these songs in the music he wrote. Grainger liked to eat brown-sugar sandwiches. He did not like to carry things, so he tied his pens, pencils, and paper to his jacket with string.

THINK! How could you use ♩ and ♫ to show the rhythm for these words: *garden, flower, rose, tulip?*

CONCEPT
MELODY
SKILLS
READ, SING, PLAY
LINKS
CULTURES, SCIENCE

The pitches you have been singing are shown on this staff. The names of these two pitches are *so* and *mi*.

These are the hand signs for *so* and *mi*.

so   mi

so

mi

This is called a **treble clef**. It shows that the pitches on the staff are in your voice range.

treble clef

So and *Mi* in Latin America

There are many countries in Latin America.
Listen to this music from Latin America.

 LISTENING CD 1:28

Tabu by Margarita Lecuona

Play along as you listen.

Playalong

Meet the Musician

Margarita Lecuona was born in Cuba. She was a songwriter, dancer, singer, and actress. She was one of the first women to write popular songs that became big hits in Cuba. She came from a musical family. Her uncle, Ernesto Lecuona, was an important Cuban composer and pianist.

In this song, one line has only *so* and *mi*. Can you find it?

RIQUI RAN

Sawing Song

CD 1:29

Latin American
Folk Song
English Words
by Linda Worsley

do

Spanish: A - se - rrín,   a - se - rrán,
English: Saw - ing wood, saw - ing wood,

los   ma - de - ros   de   San   Juan,
lum - ber - men   in   old   San   Juan,

co - men que - so,   co - men pan.
Eat - ing cheese and   eat - ing bread.

Los   de   Ri - que   al - fe - ñi - que,
Some   of   them eat   sug - ar can - dy,

los   de   Ro - que   al - fan - do - que.
some   of   them eat   gin - ger can - dy.

Ri - qui,   ri - que,   ri - qui, ran.
Ri - qui,   ri - qui,   ri - qui, ran.

Learn About Latin America

This song is well known in many places in Latin America. Latin America includes Mexico, the countries of the Caribbean, and South America.

MAP

UNITED STATES

LATIN AMERICA

Latin America is full of many wonders. It has the tallest waterfall in the world (Venezuela), the longest country (Chile), and volcanoes. In South America, people grow cacao trees, from which we get chocolate.

cacao tree ▲

21

CONCEPT
RHYTHM
SKILLS
PLAY, READ, SING
LINKS
CULTURES, DANCE, FINE ART

Play the rhythm of the sparrows' song.

Playalong

Chi chi pa pa, chi pa pa!

MAP

UNITED STATES   JAPAN

Chichipapa

The Sparrows' Singing School

CD 1:33

Music by Ryutaro Hirota
Words by Katsura Shimizu
Arranged by Kyoko Takahashi

Japanese: すずめ の がっ こう の せん せい は
English: Teach-er of the spar - rows'___ sing - ing school,

む ち を ふり ふり ちい ぱっ ぱ
Waves a stick to lead us sing-ing Chi pa pa.

せい と の すずめ は わ に なっ て
We___ stu-dents step and move to form___ a ring,

Learning about music helps us understand people around the world.

Japanese instruments from long ago are still played today. What instruments can you name that are like these?

CD-ROM

Use **World Instruments CD-ROM** to learn more about Japanese instruments.

shakuhachi ▶

samisen ▼

koto ▼

taiko drum ▶

ぢ　く　ち　を　そ　ろ　え　て　　ちい　　ぱっ　　ぱ
And we learn to sing to-geth-er　　Chi　　pa　　pa.

ちい　　ちい　　ぱっ　　ぱ　　　ちい　　ぱっ　　ぱ
Chi　　chi　　pa　　pa,　　chi　　pa　　pa!

Play Rhythm Instruments

Many musical instruments play only rhythm.
Which rhythm instruments have you played?

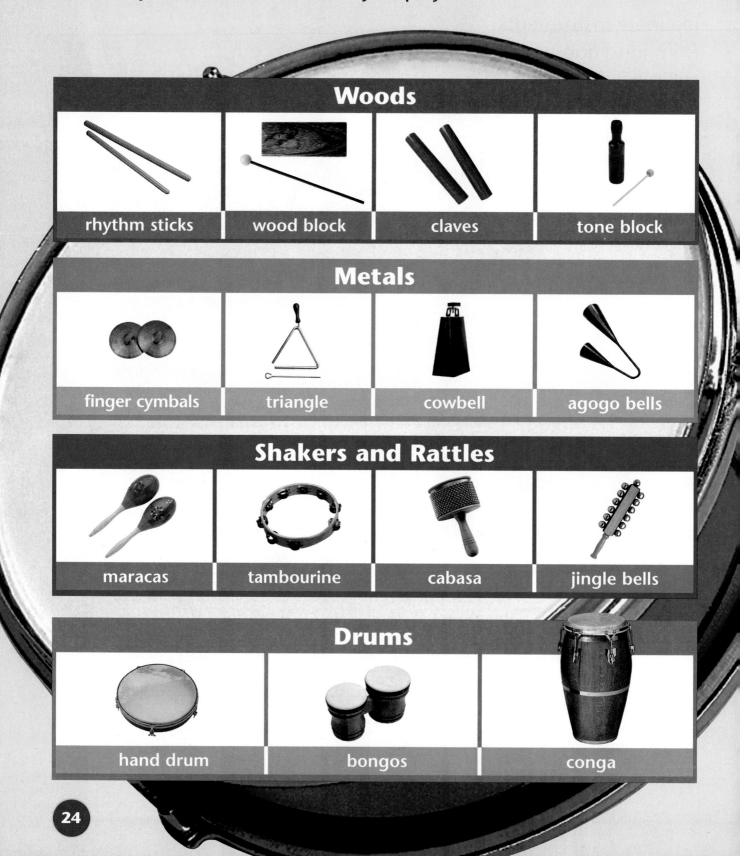

Woods

rhythm sticks | wood block | claves | tone block

Metals

finger cymbals | triangle | cowbell | agogo bells

Shakers and Rattles

maracas | tambourine | cabasa | jingle bells

Drums

hand drum | bongos | conga

Read this rhythm. Play it on wood instruments.

Playalong

Play the rhythm along with ballet music.

 LISTENING   CD 2:1

Ballet Music
by Christoph Gluck

Ballet is a type of dance.
The dancers must work
hard and be very
strong. They wear
special shoes.

New York ▶
City Ballet

Art Gallery

Little Dancer of Fourteen
by Edgar Degas

**Degas loved the ballet. He spent many
hours watching it. He is known for his
many pictures and sculptures of
ballet dancers.**

25

Loud and Soft in Music

CONCEPT
DYNAMICS
SKILLS
MOVE, SING,
PLAY
LINKS
SCIENCE,
READING

CD-ROM

Use **MIDIsaurus**
CD-ROM to practice
piano and *forte*.

Different levels of loud and soft in music are called **dynamics**. In music the word for loud is **forte**. The word for soft is **piano**.

 LISTENING   **CD 2:2**

Gavotte fantastique by Amy Beach

Move to show *forte* and *piano* in this music. Use large movements to show *forte* and small movements to show *piano*.

On the music page, f stands for *forte* and p stands for *piano*. Find the f and p in the song.

Sing about a baby beluga whale. Follow the dynamics marked in the music.

Baby Beluga

CD 2:3

Words and Music by
Raffi and D. Pike

Verse

1. Ba - by be - lu - ga in the deep blue sea,
2. Way down___ yon - der where the dol - phins play,
3. When it's___ dark, and you're___ home and fed,

Swim so wild and you swim so free.
Where you dive and___ splash all day,
Curl up snug in your wa - ter bed.

Heav - en a - bove and the sea be - low
Waves_ roll in and the waves roll out.
Moon_ is shin - ing and the stars are out.

End

And a lit - tle white whale on the go.
See the wa - ter squirt-in' out of your_ spout.
Good_ night_ lit-tle whale, good_ night.

Refrain

f

Ba - by_ be - lu - ga._ Oh, ba - by_ be - lu - ga._

p

Is the wa - ter warm? Is your ma - ma home with
Sing your lit - tle song; Sing for all your friends. We
With to - mor-row's sun, an-o - ther day's be - gun, You'll

(Last time repeat Verse 1 to End)

you so hap - py?_
like to hear you._
soon be wak - ing._

Speak and Play Louder and Softer

Say the poem with the dynamics shown.

Loose Tooth

Anonymous

CD 2:6

f I had a loose tooth, a *p* wig - gly, jig - gly

loose tooth, *f* I had a loose tooth,

p hang - ing by a thread. *f* So I pulled my

loose tooth, this *p* wig - gly, jig - gly loose tooth, And

put it 'neath my pil - low, and then I went to

bed. *f* The fair - ies took my loose tooth, *p* my

wig - gly, jig - gly loose tooth, *f* So now I have a

quar - ter and a hole in my head.

Play these instruments when you speak these words.

loose tooth

wiggly, jiggly

quarter

hole

head

Play Pitched Instruments

CONCEPT
MELODY
SKILLS
READ,
IMPROVISE, PLAY
LINKS
SCIENCE

Carl Orff was a German composer and teacher. He designed these musical instruments for students.

LOG ON

See **music.mmhschool.com** to learn more about Orff instruments.

Bass

Metallophone

Metallophone

Alto Xylophone

These instruments play different pitches.
Can you tell which is the highest? The lowest?
How do you know?

soprano
xylophone

alto
xylophone

bass
xylophone

soprano
glockenspiel

alto
glockenspiel

soprano
metallophone

alto
metallophone

bass
metallophone

Play *So* and *Mi*

So and *mi* can be in different places on the staff.
So is always on the line or space above *mi*.

Find *so* and *mi* in **"Lemonade."**

Here we come (Where from?) New York. (What's your trade?) Lem-on-ade.

(Give us some.) Have none. (Get to work and make us some.)

Play instruments with "Lemonade."

Soprano Glockenspiel

Bass Xylophone

32

Find *so* and *mi* in this song.
Play *so* and *mi* each time you say *"toot toot."*

She'll Be Comin' 'Round the Mountain

CD 2:9

Southern Mountain Song

1. She'll be com-in' 'round the moun-tain when she comes, *(toot toot)*
2. She'll be driv-ing six white hor-ses when she comes, *(whoa back, toot toot)*

She'll be com-in' 'round the moun-tain when she comes, *(toot toot)*
She'll be driv-ing six white hor-ses when she comes, *(whoa back, toot toot)*

She'll be com - in' 'round the moun - tain,
She'll be driv - ing six white hor - ses,

She'll be com - in' 'round the moun - tain,
She'll be driv - ing six white hor - ses,

She'll be com-in' 'round the moun-tain when she comes. *(toot toot)*
She'll be driv-ing six white hor-ses when she comes. *(whoa back, toot toot)*

3. Oh, we'll all go out to meet her . . . *(hi there, whoa back, toot toot)*
4. Oh, we'll all have chicken and dumplings . . . *(yum yum, etc.)*
5. She will have to sleep with Grandma . . . *(snoring sound, etc.)*

33

CONCEPT
TONE COLOR
SKILLS
SING, DESCRIBE, COMPOSE
LINKS
READING, CULTURES, SCIENCE

Read this poem out loud. Use your voice to show the meaning.

Together

Because we do
All things together,
All things improve,
Even weather.

Our daily meat
And bread taste better,
Trees are greener,
Rain is wetter.

—Paul Engle

Listen to instruments playing together in this song. What type of instrument do you hear?

MAP
UNITED STATES
GERMANY

Ach, du lieber Augustin
The More We Get Together

CD 2:12

German Folk Song

German: Ach, du lie-ber Au-gus-tin, Au-gus-tin, Au-gus-tin.
English: The more we get to-geth-er, to-geth-er, to-geth-er. The

Ach, du lie-ber Au-gus-tin, Al-les ist hin!
more we get to-geth-er, the hap-pier we'll be!

Geld ist hin, Mä-dl ist hin, Al-les ist hin, Au-gus-tin.
For your friends are my_ friends, and my_ friends are your friends. The

Ach, du lie-ber Au-gus-tin, Al-les ist hin!
more we get to-geth-er, the hap-pier we'll be!

Found Sounds!

Almost anything can be a musical instrument if it is played musically!

◀ *Scrap Arts Music is a percussion group. They use instruments made from objects they have "found."*

LISTENING CD 2:16

Assembly Required by Gregory Kozak

Listen to the music. Can you tell what the musicians are using for instruments?

Meet the Musician

Gregory Kozak is a Canadian musician. He writes music and makes the instruments for Scrap Arts Music to play. He uses everything from pieces of old large machines to drain pipes.

RECORDED INTERVIEW CD 2:17

Listen to Gregory Kozak talk about Scrap Arts Music.

Create with Found Sounds

Find things at home to use as musical instruments. How do your instruments sound different from brass instruments?

Recycle for Sound

Create music for your found sounds.

1. Create a rhythm pattern using ♩ and ♫

2. Create a melody by adding *so* and *mi* to your pattern.

3. Play found sounds on the 𝄽

4. Perform your melody twice.

5. Say the first verse of the poem "Together" at the beginning and in between each melody.

This is really working together through music!

Spotlight Your Success!

REVIEW

1 Which word means how high or low a sound is?

   a. beat   **b.** pitch

2 Which word means the short and long sounds in a song?

   a. rhythm   **b.** beat

3 Which is the hand sign for *so*?

   a.   **b.**

READ AND LISTEN

1 **Read** these rhythms. Then **listen**. Which rhythm do you hear?

2 **Move** to show when each melody goes up and down. Then **listen**. Which melody do you hear?

THINK!

1. How are beat and rhythm different?

2. Which instrument plays higher pitches? How do you know?

3. **Sing** "I'm Gonna Sing" and move your hands higher and lower to show the melody. How do the hand movements help you know where the pitches are?

4. **Write** about a song you like. Tell why you like it.

CREATE AND PERFORM

1. **Create** your own melody using *so* and *mi*.

2. Clap this rhythm.

3. Choose one pitch for each note. Do not choose pitches for the rests.

4. **Sing** your melody.

Meet the Musician
ON NATIONAL RADIO!

Name: Carol Jantsch   Age: 17
Instrument: Tuba
Home Town: Worthington, Ohio

It takes a lot of strength to play an instrument as big as a tuba. Seventeen-year-old Carol Jantsch says you need to have very strong lungs to play well. "Tuba players use breathing bags and special tools to help them improve their breathing."

Carol started playing the tuba in seventh grade. She chose to play tuba because she liked its low, loud sound. Carol had fun playing a piece called "The Flight of the Bumblebee" while dressed from head to toe in a giant bumblebee suit!

LISTENING   CD 2:19–20   **RECORDED INTERVIEW**

The Flight of the Bumblebee
by Nikolai Rimsky-Korsakov

Listen to Carol's performance and interview on the national radio program From the Top.

Spotlight on the Cello

Music has been a part of Kathy Canning's life since she started piano lessons at age five. In fourth grade she began studying the viola, and she still plays today. Ms. Canning values everything she's learned studying music, so she works to bring music to other children.

Many New York City public schools have had their music programs cut or taken away completely. Part of Ms. Canning's job is to ask for donations so schools can pay music teachers again. She also shows people how important music is.

"Kids need to learn music," she explains, because "it requires you to think and develop many skills that help you learn other subjects."

Did You Know?

The cello is one of the largest members of the string family. Because longer strings make lower sounds, a cello's pitches are deep and full.

The cello is so big that cellists have to play sitting down. They balance the instrument between their legs while playing.

LISTENING CD 2:21–22

Gavotte from Suite No. 5 for Cello
by Johann Sebastian Bach

Piano Concerto No. 2, Third Movement
by Johannes Brahms

Listen to these two pieces for cello by Bach and Brahms. Bach wrote several pieces for cello alone, without any other instruments playing along. Brahms wrote this songlike solo for cello as part of a piano concerto.

Musical Friends

Sharing music with friends is fun.

Coming Attractions

Sing in $\frac{3}{4}$ at a baseball game.

Help a doggie find his bone on *mi*, *so*, and *la*.

Perform a clog dance in AB form.

Making music can be more fun when you share it with friends.

LISTENING CD 2:23

You've Got a Friend in Me

by Randy Newman

Listen to a song about being a good friend.

Sing the song with your friends.

You've Got a Friend in Me

from the movie *Toy Story*

CD 2:24

Words and Music by Randy Newman

1. You've got a friend in me.

You've got a friend in me.

When the road looks rough a-head and you're miles

and miles from your nice warm bed,

The Opposite of Two

What is the opposite of two?
A lonely me, a lonely you.
—*Richard Wilbur*

THINK! What are some ways you and your friends can help each other when you make music together?

you just re-mem-ber what your old pal said.___

Son, you've___ got a friend in me.

Yeah, you've_ got a friend in me.

(Freely)

2. You've got a friend in me.
   You've got a friend in me.
   You got troubles, then I got 'em too.
   There isn't anything I wouldn't do for you.
   If we stick together we can see it through,
   'cause you've got a friend in me.
   Yeah, you've got a friend in me.

CONCEPT
RHYTHM
SKILLS
PERFORM,
LISTEN, PLAY
LINKS
MATH,
CULTURES

Singing can help us say how we feel.
Pat with the beat as you sing this happy song.

CD 3:1

Words and Music by Hap Palmer

Joy,   I feel the joy   of   mu - sic.

Joy,   I feel the joy   of   rhy - thm, —   and my

heart it   starts sing - ing.— And my   bod - y   starts sway - ing—

ev - 'ry - time— I   feel the joy   of   mu - sic.—

When you sing, you pat with the beat. All beats are not the same. Some are stronger than others. Beats are usually grouped in sets of stronger and weaker beats.

Sometimes beats are grouped in sets of two.

1   **2**

LISTENING CD 3:4

So Glad I'm Here Arranged by Bernice Johnson Reagon, learned from Bessie Jones

Listen to Sweet Honey in The Rock sing this song.

Pat with the beat as you listen. Are the beats in sets of two?

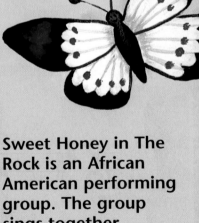

Sweet Honey in The Rock is an African American performing group. The group sings together without any accompaniment. These singers have performed together all over the world.

47

What's the Meter?

Here is a song from a two-island nation in the Caribbean called Trinidad and Tobago. **Sing** the song. **Pat** only on beat one.

Me Stone

MAP

UNITED STATES

TRINIDAD AND TOBAGO

CD 3:5

Folk Song from Trinidad and Tobago

o = pick-up
x = pass

do

Me stone is me stone, Miss Ma - ry.

Me stone is me stone, Miss Ma - ry. Me stone is me

stone, Miss Ma - ry. Pass 'em down is me stone, Miss Ma - ry.

A **meter signature** shows how many beats are in each set. A meter signature with a 2 on top has one strong beat and one weak beat in each set.

Find the $\frac{2}{?}$ meter signature at the beginning of "Me Stone." **Play** along on instruments. Play only on the strong beat.

Playalong

Sing the song again and play a passing game. Pass the stone only on the strong beat.

CONCEPT
MELODY
SKILLS
SING, IDENTIFY,
PLAY
LINKS
CULTURES,
FINE ART

Sing this funny song about a donkey named Tinga Layo. Can you find *mi* and *so* in the song?

MAP

UNITED
STATES

WEST INDIES

TINGA LAYO

CD 3:8

West Indies Calypso Song
English Words by Merrill Staton

Refrain

do

Spanish: Ting - a   Lay - o!   Ay, mi bu - rri - to, ven;
English: Ting - a   Lay - o!   Come, lit - tle don - key, come;

1., 2.   (To Verse)

Ting - a   Lay - o!   Ay, mi bu - rri - to, ven.
Ting - a   Lay - o!   Come, lit - tle don - key, come.

One of the first four notes of the song is a new pitch. **Sing** the words *Tinga Layo*. On what part of the donkey's name does the new pitch come? **Move** to show how the melody moves higher and lower.

mi so **?** so

Tin - ga Lay - o!

The new pitch is **la**. It is always one step higher than *so*.

Sing "Tinga Layo" again. Use pitch syllables with hand signs instead of the donkey's name.

la

3.   *(End)* | **Verse**

Ay, mi   bu - rri - to,   ven.   1. Bu - rri - to
Come, lit - tle don - key, come.   1. My don - key

sí, bu - rri - to no, bu - rri - to   co - me con te - ne - dor.
yes, my don-key no, My don-key   sit when I   say to go.

2. My donkey haw, my donkey gee,
   My donkey don't do a thing for me.
   Refrain

3. My donkey balk, my donkey bray,
   My donkey won't hear a thing I say.
   Refrain

51

Move with a Melody

Before we had electricity, mills were used to grind corn and flour for baking. Find *mi, so,* and *la* in this song about a mill. **Sing** the song using pitch syllables and hand signs.

This pattern sounds like a mill wheel turning. **Play** it on wood instruments as you sing the song.

LISTENING CD 3:15

Moulinet (Polka) by Josef Strauss

A *moulinet* is a type of mill. Listen for the sounds of the mill.

Listen to "Moulinet" and follow the map.

Listening Map for *Moulinet*

Introduction   A   B   A   C   A   B   A   Coda

Art Gallery

The Mill
by Rembrandt van Rijn

Rembrandt van Rijn was a Dutch artist. He painted pictures of people and the Dutch countryside.

CONCEPT
RHYTHM
SKILLS
PERFORM,
LISTEN, SING
LINKS
PHYSICAL
EDUCATION

Have you ever seen a dragon? **Listen** to see if you can hear an instrument playing dragon music.

LISTENING CD 3:16

Prelude to Act II of *Siegfried*
by Richard Wagner

Sing this song about a friendly dragon.

Puff, the Magic Dragon

CD 3:17
Verse

Words and Music by
Peter Yarrow and Leonard Lipton

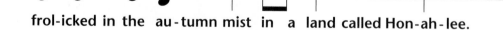
1. Puff, the mag-ic drag-on, lived by the sea and

frol-icked in the au-tumn mist in a land called Hon-ah-lee.

Lit-tle Jack-ie Pa-per loved that ras-cal Puff, and

brought him strings and seal-ing wax and oth-er fan-cy stuff. Oh!

Refrain

Puff, the mag - ic drag - on, lived by the sea and frol-icked in the au-tumn mist in a land called Hon - ah - lee.

Puff, the mag - ic drag - on, lived by the sea and

1., 2., 3.

frol-icked in the au-tumn mist in a land called Hon-ah - lee. 2. To -

4.

land called Hon - ah - lee.

2. Together they would travel on a boat with billowed sail,
Jackie left a lookout perched on Puff's gigantic tail.
Noble kings and princes would bow when'er they came.
Pirate ships would low'r their flag when Puff roared out his name. Oh!
Refrain

3. A dragon lives forever, but not so little boys;
Painted wings and giant rings make way for other toys.
One gray night it happened, Jackie Paper came no more,
And Puff, that mighty dragon, he ceased his fearless roar. Oh!
Refrain

4. His head was bent in sorrow, green scales fell like rain,
Puff no longer went to play along the cherry lane.
Without his life-long friend, Puff could not be brave,
So Puff, that mighty dragon, sadly slipped into his cave. Oh!
Refrain

An Old Favorite in $\frac{3}{}$ Meter

Listen to this baseball song. Sway to the strong beat.

The meter signature for this song is

This means that beats are in sets of 3: **strong** = weak = weak.

Sing the song.

CD 3:20

Music by Albert von Tilzer
Words by Jack Norworth

Take me out to the ball game.

Take me out with the crowd.

Buy me some pea - nuts and crack - er - jack,

I don't care if we nev - er get back,

56

The Little League World Series

Let me root, root, root for the home team,

If they don't win, it's a shame,_____

For it's one, two, three strikes you're out

At the old ball game._____

57

CONCEPT
MELODY
SKILLS
READ, SING,
LISTEN
LINKS
READING,
SCIENCE,
CULTURES

Dogs, dogs everywhere! What is your favorite kind?

Dalmatian

The Hairy Dog

My dog's so furry I've not seen
His face for years and years:
His eyes are buried out of sight,
I only guess his ears.

When people ask me for his breed,
I do not know or care:
He has the beauty of them all
Hidden beneath his hair.

—Herbert Asquith

Hungarian Sheepdog (Puli)

Maybe we cannot see this dog's eyes. We can see some of his favorite bones! Find notes in "Doggie, Doggie" that match the way these bones are arranged.

Airedale

Labrador Retriever

Beagle

Read the pitches of this song using *mi, so,* and *la.*
Sing the song with your friends.

Doggie, Doggie

CD 3:23

Singing Game

Dog - gie, dog - gie, where's your bone?

Some - one stole it from my home!

Who stole the bone?___ I stole the bone.___

59

Mi, So, La in Mexico

Mariachi bands are from Mexico.
Listen to this band play.

LISTENING CD 3:26

Chango Guango
by Tinker Villarreal and Juan Ortiz

Sing this song from Mexico.

MAP

UNITED STATES MEXICO

A la rueda de San Miguel

CD 3:27 **To the Wheel of San Miguel**

Traditional Mexican Folk Song

Spanish: 1. A la rue - da la rue - da de San Mi - guel,
English: 1. In the cir - cle, the cir - cle of *San Mi - guel,*

G

San Mi - guel, to - dos tra - en su ca - ja de miel;
San Mi - guel, Bring a box full of hon - ey to sell.

A lo ma - du - ro, a lo ma - du - ro
Wait till it ri - pens, wait till it ri - pens.

que se vol te - e Pan - cho de bu - rro.
You play the bur - ro, *Heather turn a - round now!

60 (2.) * insert any name

Carlos Chávez is an important Mexican composer. He was proud of the Indian heritage of his country. Chávez wrote *Sinfonía india* for orchestra and native Mexican instruments.

Sing this *mi so la* pattern.

Listen for the trumpet playing this pattern in the music.

CD-ROM

Use *World Instruments* **CD-ROM** to learn more about instruments in Mexico.

LISTENING CD 3:31

Sinfonía india
by Carlos Chávez

▼ Mariachi bands travel from place to place, playing their music wherever they are invited!

Call and Response

Follow the leader in this yummy song! Learn this song by listening, without looking at the music.

Pizza, Pizza, Daddy-O

CD 4:1

African American Singing Game

Leader   *Group*

An-nie has a boy-friend, Piz - za, piz - za, dad-dy - o,

Leader   *Group*

How do you know it? Piz - za, piz - za, dad - dy - o,

Leader   *Group*

'Cause she told me, Piz - za, piz - za, dad - dy - o,

Pick a leader. **Sing** the song and do the movements.

Pizza,   pizza,   dad-   dy-   o!

Leader   *Group*

Let's rope it!   Rope it, rope__ it, dad-dy - o,
Let's swim it!   Swim it, swim__ it, dad-dy - o,
Let's duck it!   Duck it, duck__ it, dad-dy o,

Leader   *Group*

Let's twist it!   Twist it, twist__ it, dad-dy - o,

Leader   *Group*

Let's end it!   End it, end__ it, dad-dy - o!

Global Voices

Follow the Leader

Get ready to sing and move with this song from Aotearoa, which is Maori for New Zealand.

New Zealand is one of a group of islands called Polynesia in the South Pacific.

Poi is the Maori word for "ball." The "long poi" is a ball tied to a long string. The string is about three feet long.

Many years ago the Maori men were known as brave warriors. They used the poi to build strength for fighting battles. Maori women also used the poi to be strong. Maori people are modern, but are proud of their traditional ways.

Maori canoe

Listen to this greeting song. The leader is calling everyone to get your poi ready and bring your canoe. **Sing** and move with it.

KIA ORA

CD 4:4

MAP

UNITED STATES

NEW ZEALAND

Leader 1: Kia ora ra toru wha

All: Kia ora ra e ngä iwi e
Tau mai ra ngä manuhiri e
Mauria mai ngä waka
Kia mätou e tu nei
Te ropu te Whanau Awhina*
karanga haere mai.

* *Whanau Awhina* is a school group.

Speak a little Maori.

Hello   Kia ora

How are you?   E pehea ana koe

Good will to you.   Tëna koutou...

canoe   Waka

Maori children in New Zealand practice a song.

LESSON
6

CONCEPT
FORM

SKILLS
SING, IDENTIFY, PERFORM

LINKS
FINE ART, CULTURES

AB Form

What do you think it is like to be a cowboy?
Listen to part of a cowboy song, then **sing** it.

LISTENING CD 4:5

Strawberry Roan
sung by Cowboy Ed McCurdy

American Cowboy Song

CD 4:6

1. I came in-to town just to spend some time,
2. "You've guessed me just right! I'm your man," I claim,
3. I jumped on his back and I held the reins,

For I had no mon-ey, not e-ven a dime;
"Do you have a wild horse you'd like me to tame?"
That straw-ber-ry horse threw me off for my pains;

Then a fel-low stepped up and he said, "I sup-pose
Well, he said that he had, and a bad one to buck,
So I climbed on a-gain to the horse-'s sur-prise,

You're a bronc-bust-ing cow-boy by the looks of your clothes."
And for throw-ing good rid-ers, the__ horse had good luck.
And he tried then to throw me right_ up to the skies.

What is the form of "Strawberry Roan"?
What is a *Strawberry Roan*?

Listen to this music that sounds like it is from the old West.

🎵 **LISTENING** | CD 4:9

Round-up by Elie Siegmeister

🎨 *Art Gallery*

Bronco Buster by Frederic Remington

Frederic Remington is an American artist. He is famous for his Western art.

Refrain

Well, it's oh, that straw-ber-ry roan!_____

Oh, that straw-ber-ry roan,_____

That straw-ber-ry pon-y no one ev-er rode,

And the cow-boy that tries it is sure to get thrown.

Oh, that straw-ber-ry roan!_____

Folk Dancing in AB Form

In pioneer times, people danced to music of a string band. This style of music is called oldtime.

Clog dancing is done to oldtime music.

Perform a clog-dance step: Brush one toe forward and back. Then step firmly on that same foot. Repeat with the other foot.

LISTENING CD 4:10

Clog (Oldtime Music)

Walk to the A section. Clog step to the B section of this music.

What is the form of this American folk song?
Sing the song and move to it.

CD 4:11

Willowbee

American Folk Song

Ⓐ **Refrain**

This way we wil-low-bee, oh, wil-low-bee, oh, wil-low-bee,

End (Fine)

This way we wil-low-bee, all day____ long.

Verse Ⓑ

Oh,____ Danc-ing down the al-ley, the al-ley, the al-ley,

Go back to the beginning and sing to the End (Da Capo al Fine)

Danc-ing down the al-ley, All day long. Oh,____

THINK!

How can you tell if a song is in AB form?

69

CONCEPT
TONE COLOR
SKILLS
COMPARE,
CREATE, PLAY
LINKS
CULTURES,
HISTORY

How does a trumpet sound different from a piano? The **tone color** of an instrument or voice is its special quality of sound. Tone quality is what makes one instrument sound different from another.

Listen for the tone color of the trumpet in this song. Many Jewish people from Eastern Europe sing this song.

MAP

UNITED
STATES

EASTERN EUROPE

Klezmer Band

Chirri Bim

CD 4:14

Traditional Yiddish Song

Chir - ri bim, chir - ri bom, Chir - ri

bim bom bim bom bom._____ Chir - ri bim, chir - ri

bom, chir - ri bim bom bim bom bom.

Listen to the tone color of instruments in your class. **Compare** how they are different.

Create an accompaniment for the song. Use different tone colors.

Ⓑ

Ai chir – ri bir – ri bir – ri, ai chir – ri bir – ri bir – ri,

ai chir – ri bir – ri bir – ri, ai chir – ri bir – ri,

ai chir – ri bir – ri bir – ri, ai chir – ri bir – ri bir – ri,

chir – ri bir – ri bim bom bom.

The Color of Brass Instruments

Trumpets are made of brass tubing. A mouthpiece fits into the tubing.

Brass players buzz their lips as they blow into the mouthpiece. This makes the sound. Try buzzing to make a sound!

Brass Instruments

trumpet

tuba

French horn

trombone

euphonium

The trumpet is the smallest and highest-pitched brass instrument. It has the brightest tone color. **Listen** and compare the tone color of the other brass instruments.

THINK! Which instrument do you think plays the lowest pitches? Why?

A **concerto** is a work written to show the skill of a solo performer. Some concertos are written for two or more soloists.

🔊 **LISTENING** | CD 4:17

Allegro from Concerto for Two Trumpets by Antonio Vivaldi

This concerto is for two solo trumpets and an orchestra.

Point to what you hear as you **listen**.

CD-ROM

Use *Orchestral Instruments* **CD-ROM** to learn more about brass instruments.

Listening Map for *Concerto for Two Trumpets*

Meet the Musician

Antonio Vivaldi composed music for a school for orphaned girls. The school became famous for its good orchestra. Vivaldi wrote over 400 concertos.

CONCEPT
FORM
SKILLS
IDENTIFY, PLAY,
COMPOSE
LINKS
READING,
CULTURES,
FINE ART

Have you ever been to summer camp? Here is a song you might sing at camp.

A Pat on the Back

CD 4:18

American Folk Song

Swing 𝄋

Oh, give your friend a pat on the back, a pat on the back, a

pat on the back, and say to your friend be -

End (Fine)

fore the day's end, "We've had a good day___ to - day."

Yes - ter - day was most - ly trou - ble and sor - row,

Go back to the sign and sing to the End (D.S. al Fine)

No-bod-y knows what's apt to hap-pen to - mor - row. So,

D.S. al Fine means to go back to the 𝄋 sign and sing until you see the word **Fine**. **Find** the terms *D.S. al Fine* and *Fine* in the song.

A song in two sections is in AB form. How many sections does this song have? Are any sections the same? This song is in ABA form.

Sing this part. Then **play** it with the A section.

See music.mmhschool.com to research American folk songs.

Compose a Melody

The moon and owls come out at night.

Finis

Night is come,
Owls are out;
Beetles hum
Round about.
Children snore
Safe in bed,
Nothing more
Need be said.

Sir Henry Newbolt

Sing this nighttime song.

Good Night, Sleep Tight

CD 4:21

Traditional

Good night, sleep tight, friends will come to-mor-row night.

Create a "nighttime" melody to the poem "Finis." Use the pitches *mi*, *so*, and *la*.

Sing your melody as the B section after you sing "Good Night, Sleep Tight."

LISTENING CD 4:24

Child Falling Asleep
by Robert Schumann

Can you tell what is happening in the music?

Art Gallery

Ara River at Akabane, 1929
by Kawase Hasui

Kawase Hasui is a Japanese artist. He is known for his pictures of night scenes and snow. He created nearly 600 prints during his lifetime.

Learn About Music That Tells a Story

Many composers like to write music that tells a story. Often the title of the music tells what it is about.

Composers might use different tone colors and melodies to paint a musical picture.

***Scenes from Childhood* is a book of many short piano pieces. Each piece describes a different time in a child's life.**

The composer, Robert Schumann, loved to read books and poems. He also loved to play the piano. Sometimes he would compose music that was about his life and friends.

Spotlight Your Success!

REVIEW

1 Here are *so* and *mi*. Where is *la*?

so   mi

a.   b.   c.

2 Here are *so* and *mi* in different places. Where is *la* now?

so   mi

a.   b.   c.

3 Which shows $\frac{3}{?}$

1   2   1   2   3

READ AND LISTEN

1 **Read** these melodies. Then **listen**. Which is the one with *la*?

a. do

b. do

2 **Listen** to this melody and pat the strong beat.
Is it in ²₈ or ³₈?

a. ²₈   b. ³₈

THINK!

1 How are beat and strong beat different?

2 How are ²₈ and ³₈ meters different?

3 **Write** about a song or listening selection
you like. Tell what you like about the music.

CREATE AND PERFORM

1 **Create** your own melody using *mi*,
so, and *la*.

2 Use this rhythm. First, clap the rhythm.

3 Choose one pitch for each note.

4 **Sing** your melody.

Meet the Musician
ON NATIONAL RADIO!

Name: Vincent Yu **Age: 11**
Instrument: Piano
Home Town: Longmeadow, Massachusetts

Playing piano wasn't always fun for eleven-year-old Vincent Yu. When he first started to take lessons, he didn't enjoy them at all. "My mom would have to force me to play piano," he remembers. "I wanted to watch TV!"

Before long, though, Vincent started to feel differently. Once he learned how to read music and play songs, Vincent began to like his weekly lessons. He was surprised to find that playing piano had become fun!

Playing piano is Vincent's favorite activity now. "I especially like to play pieces that make me use my imagination," he says. Learning to play piano was difficult, but Vincent is glad he stuck with it.

LISTENING CD 4:26–27 **RECORDED INTERVIEW**

The Cat and the Mouse
by Aaron Copland

Listen to Vincent's performance and interview on the national radio program From the Top.

A Tip From the Top
"Stick with it!"
When learning something new or difficult, stick with it for a while. Vincent Yu found the piano got easier as he learned more about it, and he had fun playing it.

Spotlight on the Trumpet

Did You Know?

Trumpeters make their sound by pressing their lips against their instruments and blowing until their lips "buzz," or vibrate.

A trumpet player can fit a *mute*, or hollow cone, inside the trumpet's bell to play more quietly. Placing a mute inside a trumpet's bell softens its sound.

If you straightened out a trumpet from mouthpiece to bell, you would have a brass tube over four feet long.

Each time a trumpeter plays for a while, he or she must press the *spit valve* or *water key* to empty the water from the instrument. The wetness comes from the breath the player blows through the trumpet.

LISTENING CD 4:28–29

Prince of Denmark's March
by Jeremiah Clarke

Rondo for Lifey
by Leonard Bernstein

Jeremiah Clarke wrote his trumpet piece several hundred years ago. Back then, brass instruments were much simpler than they are today. They could only play a few notes.

Listen to the modern trumpet in the piece by Leonard Bernstein.

mouthpiece · keys · bell · valves · spit valve · mute

81

UNIT 3

Our Musical World

You are going on a musical journey in this unit. In every lesson you will visit a different continent and explore some of its music.

Coming Attractions

Move with the half note in Africa.

Play *do*, *mi*, and *so* in Korea.

Create "Ice Music" in Antarctica.

Listen to this song about our wonderful world. How does Louis Armstrong sing expressively? *Expressive* singing helps us know what the song means.

LISTENING CD 4:30

What a Wonderful World
by George Weiss and Bob Thiele

Sing the song expressively. Think about the words. Use dynamics and tone color to express yourself.

Louis Armstrong

What a Wonderful World

CD 4:31

Swing (♪ = ♪)

Words and Music by
George David Weiss and Bob Thiele

1. I see trees of green, red ros - es too,

I see them bloom for me and you, ___

___ and I think_ to my-self What a won-der-ful world. ___

2. I see skies of blue and clouds of white,

the bright___ bles-sed day, the dark___ sac-red night,___

___ and I think___ to my-self What a won-der-ful world.___

Yes, I think to my-self, What a won-der-ful world.___

Rhythm in North America

CONCEPT
RHYTHM
SKILLS
LISTEN, DESCRIBE, IDENTIFY
LINKS
CULTURES, SCIENCE, FINE ART

Celebrate our musical journey. Listen and pat the strong beat to a fanfare. A **fanfare** is a short piece of music that is played to salute someone or to celebrate.

 LISTENING CD 5:1

Entrance Fanfare by Robert Dickow

This fanfare is played with brass instruments. As you travel in this unit, you will learn about many instruments from different continents.

Listen to "This Is My Country" and **move** as you wave a pretend flag.

How long are your movements in each direction?

Our flag is a symbol of our country. There are symbols in music as well. The symbol for a sound two beats long is called a **half note**.

It is as long as two quarter notes put together. **Find** the half notes in this song.

This Is My Country

CD 5:2

Music by Al Jacobs
Words by Don Raye

1.-2. This is my coun-try! Land of my { birth. choice.

This is my coun-try! { Grand - est on earth. Hear my proud voice.

I pledge thee my al - le - giance, A - mer - i - ca the bold, for

This is my coun-try, to have and to hold!

Sing Half Notes in Canada

This is a well-known song in our northern neighbor, Canada. The words describe the land there. Listen for, then **find** half notes in the song.

CD 5:5

Canadian Folk Song

Verse

1. Land of the sil - ver birch, home of the bea - ver,
2. Down in the for - est, deep in the low - lands,

Where still the might - y moose wan-ders at will,
My heart cries out for thee, hills of the north,

Blue lake and rock - y shore, I will re - turn once more.
Blue lake and rock - y shore, I will re - turn once more.

Refrain

Boom de de boom boom, Boom de de boom boom,

Boom de de boom boom, Boom.

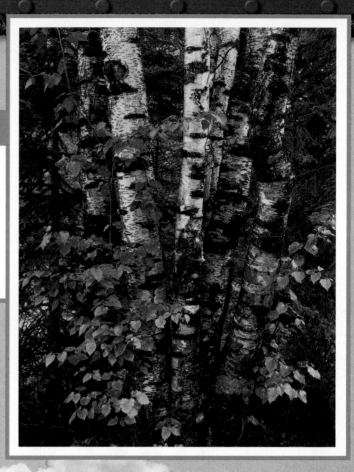

Birches from Alberta, Canada
by Saelon Renkes

Saelon Renkes has taken pictures all over the world. She loves nature and traveling. She was a member of the Peace Corps.

Choose one pattern and clap as you sing "Land of the Silver Birch."

a.

b.

A New Pitch in South America

CONCEPT
MELODY
SKILLS
LISTEN,
DESCRIBE, READ
LINKS
CULTURES

The Caribbean islands are near South America. **Listen** to *Caribbean Steel Band* play.

MAP

UNITED STATES   CARIBBEAN ISANDS

PERU   BRAZIL

BOLIVIA

LISTENING   CD 5:8

Steel Drums Jam

Pick high, middle, and low papayas to show the melody of this song.

Shake the Papaya Down

CD 5:9

Calypso Song
Collected by W. S. Haynie

do

Ma - ma says no play, This is a work - day.

Up with the bright sun, Get all the work done.

If you will help me, Climb up the tall tree,

Shake the pa - pa - ya down.

90

Look at these parrots.
The highest parrot sings *so*.
The middle one sings *mi*.
The lowest parrot sings our new pitch.

The new pitch is called **do**. Here is the hand sign for *do*:

Look at these "papaya pitches."

Sing the pitches and use hand signs.
Find the "papaya pitches" in the song.

A Carnival Song with *Do*

Brazil is on the continent of South America. Every spring, the city of Rio de Janeiro has a big carnival. **Listen** as Carmen Miranda sings this popular carnival song.

 LISTENING CD 5:12

Mama eu quero (Brazilian Carnival Song)

Listen to the same carnival song in English.

▲ **Carmen Miranda**

CD 5:13

Brazilian Carnival Song
English Version by Merrill Staton

do

1. Ma - ma Pa - qui - ta,   Ma - ma Pa - qui - ta,
2. Ma - ma Pa - qui - ta,   Ma - ma Pa - qui - ta,

Ma - ma Pa - qui - ta has no mon - ey for pa - pa - yas;
Ma - ma Pa - qui - ta has no mon - ey for pa - ja - mas;

Can't buy pa - pa - yas,   can't buy ba - nan - as;
Can't buy pa - ja - mas,   can't buy som - bre - ros;

She can - not buy pa - pa - yas or ba - nan - as. No, ma - ma - ma - ma,
She can - not buy pa - ja - mas or som - bre - ros. No, ma - ma - ma - ma,

In this song *do* is on the
added line below the staff.

so   mi   do

Find lines in the song that
have only *do*, *mi*, and *so*.
Then sing the song.

Ma - ma Pa - qui - ta,   Ma - ma Pa - qui - ta,
Ma - ma Pa - qui - ta,   Ma - ma Pa - qui - ta,

Ma - ma Pa - qui - ta will not have a ripe pa - pa - ya;
Ma - ma Pa - qui - ta will not have the fine pa - ja - mas;

No ripe pa - pa - ya,   no ripe ba - nan - a,
No fine pa - ja - mas,   no fine som - bre - ros,

So go to Car - ni - val to laugh and dance and sing.

93

Move to the Half Note in Africa

CONCEPT
RHYTHM
SKILLS
DESCRIBE, LISTEN, READ
LINKS
CULTURE, DANCE

Pata means "touch" in the Zulu and Xhosa languages. To "touch" in a dance means to put a foot or hand down lightly. **Move** to the half note as you listen to "Pata Pata."

MAP

UNITED STATES

NIGERIA

SOUTH AFRICA   ZIMBAB\[

CD-ROM

Learn more about African Instruments with *World Instruments* CD-ROM.

LISTENING   CD 5:16

Pata Pata by Miriam Makeba

Meet the Musician

Miriam Makeba is a very well-known South African singer. "Pata Pata" is like the songs she sang when she was a little girl.

She uses these traditional instruments in the song.

African shakers

mbira

Learn a hand dance to do with "Pata Pata."
Move with the music.

Beat 1

Beat 2

Beat 3

Beat 4

Beat 5

Beat 6

Beat 7

Beat 8

Beat 9

Beat 10

Beat 11

Beat 12

Beat 13

Beat 14

Beat 15

Beat 16

Half Notes in a Greeting Song

Sorida is a way to say "hello" in Zimbabwe.
Find the half notes in this song. Sing and move with the song.

Sorida

CD 5:17

Zimbabwe Greeting Song

Shona: So - ri - da! So - ri - da, ri - da ri -

da, da - da-da - da, da - da-da - da, ri - da ri -

da, da - da - da - da, da - da-da - da, ri - da ri - da!

96

Read Half Notes

Meet the Musician

Chief Fela Sowande was a tribal chief in Nigeria and a professor of music in several universities. He composed music using melodies from his country and European instruments.

Listen to the music, then learn a pattern to clap with it.

🎵 **LISTENING** CD 5:19

Akinla from *African Suite* by Fela Sowande

Read these patterns. Try them with the music.

a.

b.

This music uses only string instruments.

Learn About the String Family

The string family in an orchestra is made up of the violin, viola, cello, and double bass. Sound is produced by bowing or plucking the strings.

String Family

bow   violin   viola   cello   double bass

97

Pitches in Asia

CONCEPT
MELODY

SKILLS
PLAY, LISTEN, COMPOSE

LINKS
CULTURES, SCIENCE, FINE ART

Children in South Korea sing this song and pretend to catch the moon. **Find** *do*, *mi*, and *so* in the song.

MAP
UNITED STATES
KOREA
CHINA
INDONESIA

CD-ROM
Look at *World Instruments* **CD-ROM** to learn more about Chinese instruments.

DAL TARO KACHA
Come, Pick the Moon

CD 5:20

Music by Tae-Hyun Park
Words by Suk Joong Yoon
English Words by Linda Worsley

do

Korean: 애 들 아 나오 너 라 달 따러 가 자
English: **Chil - dren come, ev - 'ry one, Come and pick the moon.**

장 대 들고 망 태 메 고 뒷 동 산 으 로
Bring your staff and bring your knap-sack, Some-one needs it soon.

뒷 동 산에 올 라 가 무 등 을 타 고
Climb the hill, with your staff, pick the moon to - day.

장 - 대 로 달 을 따 서 망 태 에 담 자
Now put it in your knap-sack, car - ry it a - way.

China is next to Korea. This music is about a party.

LISTENING CD 5:24

Evening Party by He Luting

Listen for Chinese folk instruments.

erhu

Meet the Musician

He Luting was an important Chinese composer. He wrote music that mixed Chinese and European types of music. He also wrote many songs about China.

guzheng

yunluo

99

Compose in Indonesia

Listen to the ducks "quack." Find *do mi so*.

CD 5:25

Itik Besenda Gurau
The Ducks

Indonesian Folk Song
English Words by Linda Worsley

do

Bahasa Indonesian: Kwek, kwek, kwek; Kwek, kwek, kwek! It - ik ber - ja lan ra mai.
English: Quack, quack, quack; Quack, quack, quack! Ducks go walk-ing in a line.

Kwek, kwek, kwek; Kwek, kwek, kwek! Ri - ang be - sen - da gu - rau.
Quack, quack, quack; Quack, quack, quack! Talk-ing, walk-ing, feel-ing fine.

Ha ha ha; ha ha ha! A ku ter ta wa;
Ha ha ha; ha ha ha! Laugh-ing as they go;

Ha ha ha; ha ha ha! A ku me li hat ka mu.
Ha ha ha; ha ha ha! Ducks go walk-ing in a row.

Kwek! Kwek! Kwek, kwek, kwek! Ber sa ma ra mai.
Quack! Quack! Quack, quack, quack! Hap - py, hear them say:

Kwek! Kwek! Kwek, kwek, kwek! Me nu ju su ngai! Kwek!
Quack! Quack! Quack, quack, quack! "Let's go swim to-day, Quack!"

100

Compose your own duck music!

Here are all the measures from the song that have *do, mi,* or *so.* Sing these measures with pitch syllables and hand signs. Then sing them with "quacks."

Using any of these measures to **compose** a four-measure melody. **Sing** your duck song.

THINK! How would you change your song if you could?

Art Gallery

Two Mandarin Ducks by Ando Hiroshige

Ando Hiroshige was born in Japan. He was a fireman, like his father, as well as a painter. He made around 5,400 pictures in his life.

LESSON 5

CONCEPT
DYNAMICS
SKILLS
READ, DESCRIBE, LISTEN
LINKS
CULTURES, DANCE, SCIENCE

Crescendo in Europe!

People all over the world know that work can get done faster if it is done to music. What are the steps of making wool in this song?

MAP
UNITED STATES NORWAY SWEDEN

Sheep Shearing

CD 5:29

Swedish Folk Song
English Words by Sam Blum

Verse

1. Go get the sheep, we're clip - ping to - day,
2. Tell Moth - er dear we're card - ing to - day,

Clip - ping their wool, yes, clip - ping their wool
Card - ing the wool, yes, card - ing the wool

So we can knit some stock - ings for you,
So we can knit a scarf for her, too,

Then we shall dance 'til morn - ing.
Then we shall dance 'til morn - ing.

When music gets gradually louder, it is called **crescendo**.

crescendo

Find the *crescendo* signs shown in the song.
Sing the song, with a *crescendo* where it is shown. **Sing** the song again, adding the movement.

pat   clap   clap

Refrain   (pat   clap   clap) (pat   clap   clap)

Surr, surr, surr, surr, surr, surr, Wheel spins a-round, hear, hear the sound;

(pat   clap   clap)

Surr, surr, surr, surr, surr, surr, Then we shall dance 'til morn-ing.

3. Tell brother John we're spinning today,
   Spinning the wool, yes, spinning the wool
   So we can knit a lace for his shoe,
   Then we shall dance 'til morning.

4. Tell sister Jane we're dyeing today,
   Dyeing the wool, yes, dyeing the wool
   So we can knit a sweater of blue,
   Then we shall dance 'til morning.

Global Voices

Music from Norway

Norway is known as the land of the Midnight Sun. In Northern Norway the sun never sets during the summer months. **Listen** to a folk song from Norway.

LISTENING   **CD 6:1**

Såg du noko? Norwegian Folk Song

Speak the words of the song. It is about a man looking for his wife.

Såg du noko?
Norwegian Folk Song

Såg du noko til kjerringa mi?
Langt nord i lia i lia;
Svart hatt, stutt stakk;
Og lita gammal og låghalt;

Da di da di da da di do
Da da di da da di dai ja

Da di da di da da di do
Da da di da da di dai ja

Meet the Musician

Edvard Grieg was a composer from Norway. He used folk songs from Norway in the music he composed. When he was small, he liked to stay at home and write music more than going to school.

Do you hear the folk song "Såg du noko?" in this music?

LISTENING CD 6:2

Symphonic Dances, Op. 64, No. 4 by Edvard Grieg

Listen again and **move** to show the changing dynamics.

CONCEPT
RHYTHM
SKILLS
READ, PLAY, LISTEN
LINKS
CULTURES, SCIENCE

Australia is called the land "down under" because it lies below the equator. There are many animals in Australia. Which ones are named in the song?

LOG ON

See **music.mmhschool.com** to research musical instruments from Australia.

MAP

UNITED STATES

NEW ZEALAND

AUSTRALIA

Australia's on the Wallaby

CD 6:3

Australian Folk Song

Aus-tra-lia's on the wal-la-by, Just lis-ten to the coo-ee.

For the kan-ga-roo he rolls his swag and the e-mu shoul-ders blu-ey.

The boo-mer-angs are whiz-zing round, The din-go scratch-es grav-el.

The pos-sum bear and ban-di-coot are all up-on the trav-el.

A rest that lasts two beats is called a half rest.

Find the half notes and half rests in this pattern.

Playalong

Choose an unpitched instrument. **Play** as you sing the song.

kangaroo

bandicoot

emu

dingo

possum bear

Play Half Notes in New Zealand

Music is special to the Maori people of New Zealand. Learn to sing the song. Play half notes on rhythm sticks with a partner.

Oma Rapeti

Run, Rabbit

CD 6:6

New Zealand Folk Song
Collected and Transcribed by Kathy B. Sorensen

Maori: O-ma ra - pe-ti, o-ma ra - pe-ti, o-ma_ o-ma o-ma!_

Kau- a ri - ro kau- a ri - ro koe ai - a._

Ka o-ra i-a he-i a - ha ra-pe - ti._

O-ma ra - pe-ti, o-ma ra - pe-ti, o-ma_ o-ma o-ma!_

The *pukaea* is an early horn that is played like a trumpet. It is made from a hollow tree branch. Its sound can carry long distances. It was often used to signal a warning.

Listen for the *pukaea* in this modern music.

LISTENING CD 6:10

pukaea

Pukaea by Jaz Coleman and Hinewehi Mohi

English: Run, rab - bit, run, rab - bit, run, run, run!

Don't give_ the far - mer_ his fun, fun, fun.

He'll get by with - out his rab - bit_ pie,

so run, rab - bit, run, rab - bit, run, run, run!

109

Expressive Dynamics in Antarctica

CONCEPT
DYNAMICS
SKILLS
LISTEN,
COMPOSE, PLAY
LINKS
CULTURES,
SCIENCE,
SOCIAL STUDIES

You have been learning about many instruments. Antarctica is very cold and covered in ice. The only instrument in Antarctica is the wind itself!

Listen to music describing the Antarctic wind. Do you hear sounds of seals in the music?

LISTENING CD 6:11

Antarctica by Paul Winter

MAP

UNITED STATES

ANTARCTICA

THINK! How does the music create a feeling of being in a very cold place? If you were a composer, what different sounds would you use to create a feeling of being in a very cold place?

Crescendo means "gradually getting louder." Gradually getting softer is called **decrescendo**. Here are the symbols used in music for these two terms:

crescendo   *decrescendo*

The freezing weather creates many types of ice in Antarctica. **Create** your own "Ice Music." Choose an instrument that might sound like one of the types of ice. Use *crescendo* and *decrescendo*. **Play** your "Ice Music" along with *Antarctica*.

green growler

new frazil fibrous

pancake

pack

brash

Crescendo and Decrescendo with Penguins

Here is a funny poem about penguins. **Move** to the poem as penguins might.

Three Little Penguins

CD 6:12

Anonymous
Adapted by Marilyn Davidson

Three lit - tle pen-guins dressed in white and black.

Wad - dle, wad - dle for - ward and wad - dle right back!

Three lit - tle pen-guins, in a fun - ny pose,

They are wear - ing their eve - ning clothes.

End

Play this pattern on a triangle with the poem. Use *crescendo* and *decrescendo*.

Playalong

Their suits are black and their vests are white,

They wad-dle to the left and they wad-dle to the right.

They stand on the ice and they look ver-y neat,

Go back to the beginning and sing to the End.

As they wad-dle a - long on their lit-tle flat feet.

CONCEPT
MELODY
SKILLS
READ, PLAY, IMPROVISE
LINKS
CULTURES, SOCIAL STUDIES

Wherever we live, the earth is home for all of us. Can you name all the continents on Earth?

MAP

UNITED STATES

LATIN AMERICA

En nuestra Tierra tan linda
On Our Beautiful Planet Earth

CD 6:15

Latin American Folk Song
Adapted by José-Luis Orozco
English Words by Linda Worsley

Spanish: 1. En nues - tra Tie - rra tan lin - da_____
English: Here on our beau - ti - ful plan - et,_____

pron - to va_a sa - lir el sol,_____
soon the bright sun___ will shine,_____

pron - to va_a sa - lir el sol_____
soon the bright sun___ will shine,_____

en nues - tra Tie - rra tan lin - da._____
here on our beau - ti - ful plan - et._____

2. pronto va a soplar el viento
3. pronto va a caer la lluvia
4. pronto brillará una estrella

2. soon a fresh wind will blow,
3. soon a warm rain will fall
4. soon a bright star will glow

Sing and move to this song.

Earth   sun   wind   rain   stars

Find *do*, *mi*, and *so* in this music.
Sing it with pitch syllables and hand
signs. **Play** it as you sing the song.

Glockenspiel

Improvise with *Do Mi So*

Listen to another song about our world.

LISTENING CD 6:21

MIDI

For another activity with "He's Got the Whole World in His Hands," see *Spotlight on MIDI*.

He's Got the Whole World in His Hands
Sung by opera singer Leontyne Price

Find *so mi do* in this song. Sing the song.

He's Got the Whole World in His Hands

CD 6:22

Freely

Traditional Spiritual

1. He's got the whole world in His hands.
   He's got the whole world in His hands.
   He's got the whole world in His hands.
   He's got the whole world in His hands.

2. He's got the wind and the rain in His hands.
   He's got the sun and the moon in His hands.
   He's got the wind and the rain in His hands.
   He's got the whole world in His hands.

3. He's got you and me, brother, in His hands.
   He's got you and me, sister, in His hands.
   He's got you and me, brother, in His hands.
   He's got the whole world in His hands.

Choose a continent and write about it.
Improvise a melody using the pitches *do*, *mi*, and *so* to complete one of the phrases below.
Sing your melody and have others guess which continent.

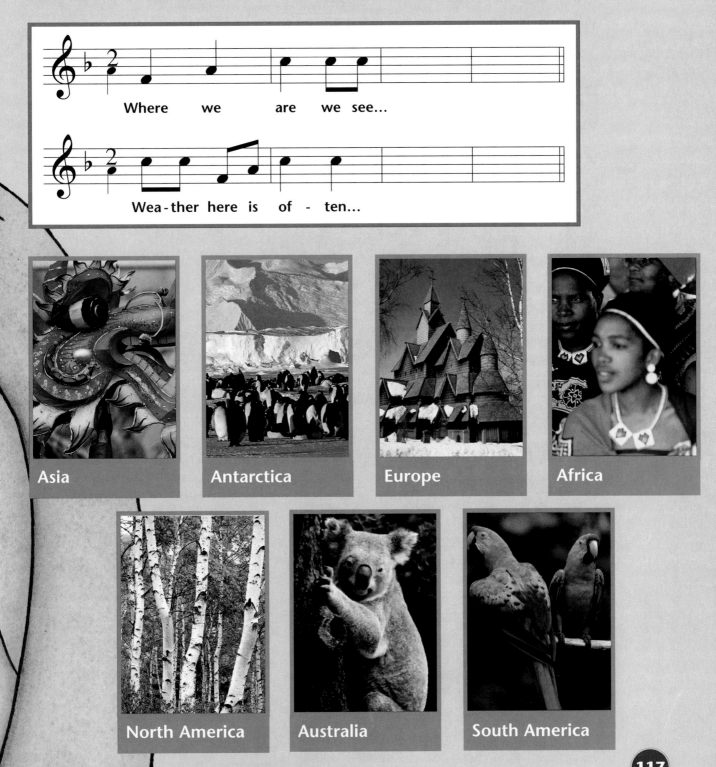

Where   we   are   we   see...

Wea-ther here is of - ten...

Asia

Antarctica

Europe

Africa

North America

Australia

South America

Spotlight Your Success!

REVIEW

1 Here are *so* and *mi*. Where is *do*?

a. around the third line
b. in the second space
c. around the line below the staff

2 Which instrument belongs to the brass family?

a.

b.

READ AND LISTEN

1 Read these melodies. Then **listen**. Which melody uses *so mi do*?

a.
do

b.
do

2 **Read** these rhythms. Then **listen** and pat with the strong beat. Which do you hear?

a.

b.

 THINK!

1 How is a half note different from a quarter note?

2 As you traveled in this unit, you learned about many instruments from different continents. Suppose you could learn to play any instrument from any country. Which instrument would you choose? Why?

3 **Write** about a song you like. Tell what you like about the music.

CREATE AND PERFORM

1 **Create** your own melody using *do*, *mi*, and *so*. Use this rhythm for your melody.

   1. **Clap** this rhythm.

   2. Choose one pitch for each note.

2 **Sing** your melody.

Music News

Meet the Musician

ON NATIONAL RADIO!

Name: Bianca Garcia
Age: 13
Instrument: Flute
Home Town: Salem, New Hampshire

Thirteen-year-old flutist Bianca Garcia likes to challenge herself. When she goes swimming, she likes to see how long she can hold her breath under water. When she goes skiing, she likes to go straight down the hill. She spent hours trying to tie her shoes before she could even walk!

Bianca also challenges herself through music. "I like to play difficult pieces the most," she says. Bianca pushes herself to be the best musician she can be.

LISTENING   CD 6:26–27   **RECORDED INTERVIEW**

Concerto for Flute and Orchestra, Allegro
by Jacques Ibert

Listen to Bianca's performance and interview on the national radio program **From the Top**.

Spotlight on the String Quartet

Did You Know?

A string quartet is made up of two violins, a viola, and a cello.

The first violin leads the group and starts the music with a signal from his or her bow.

One or both violins usually play the main melodies in a string quartet. The viola and cello play lower-sounding parts, giving the group a fuller sound.

Composers have been writing music for the string quartet since about 1750.

LISTENING CD 6:28–29

String Quartet No. 2 in D Minor
by Franz Josef Haydn

String Quartet No. 2
by Béla Bartók

Listen to the beautiful melody in this string quartet by Haydn. Many years after Haydn, Bartók wrote string quartets that substituted exciting sound effects for melodies.

UNIT
4

Your Turn, My Turn

You will get to take turns singing, playing, and moving in this unit.

Your turn.

I'm next.

Coming Attractions

Sing and make shoes on *do, re, mi, so.*

Fly a kite with dotted half notes.

Move to a Round Dance.

UNIT 4

Imagine that it is early morning and the sun is just out of sight. Let's take turns waking it up!

 CD 7:1

Words by John Jacobson
Music by Emily Crocker

Refrain

Wake up the sun___ so the day can come.
Wake up the sun___ so the day can come.

Rest now the sil - ver - y moon.
Put 'way the moon___ and the stars.

Dark - ness has gone___ and the light has won.
This is the time___ now so ev - 'ry - one,

Morn - ing will be___ here soon.
come for this day___ will be ours.

124

Verse

1. Shad-ows will van - ish, dew dis-ap-pear,___
2. She might be shy_____ like you and I,_____

the world can be - gin___ a - new.
wait - ing so long___ to grow.

Each day a new___ start, year af - ter year.___
She'll hes - i - tate,_____ she'll make us wait.___

(Repeat Refrain after Verse 1)

Now let the sun shine through, for you!
Now's the time to show your glow!

Coda *(last time only)*

Some - bo - dy wake the sun.

LESSON 1

Celebrating with $\frac{3}{4}$ Rhythm

CONCEPT
RHYTHM
SKILLS
DESCRIBE,
LISTEN, PLAY
LINKS
CULTURES,
FINE ART

Welcome to a party! What ways are people taking turns at this party? Take turns singing this song.

Find the meter for this song. How many beats are in one measure of $\frac{3}{4}$?

HELLO, HELLO THERE

from the musical *Bells Are Ringing*

CD 7:4

Music by Jule Styne
Words by Betty Comden and Adolph Green

A

Group 1   *Group 2*

Hel - lo,   hel - lo,   there.   Hi!

All

Pleased to   meet you!   It's a pleas-ure   and a priv'-lege!

*End
(Fine)*

Glad to   know you!   How are you? Hel - lo!

The oboe and violin will take turns playing in this music. **Listen** for beats in sets of three. **Move** when the oboe plays.

Learn more about the violin and the oboe on **Orchestral Instruments CD-ROM**.

LISTENING CD 7:7

Adagio from Concerto for Violin and Oboe
by Johann Sebastian Bach

B

Group 1

Well,   well,   what   do   you   know?

Group 2

We should have done this a long time a - go!

Group 1

Well,   well,   is - n't   it   swell!

Go back to the beginning and sing to the End (Da Capo al Fine)

Group 2

Is - n't   it   nice   to   say:

127

Clap and Play to 3

Sounds lasting three beats are shown with a **dotted half note**. The dot adds one beat to the half note. **Find** the dotted half notes in this song.

MAP

UNITED STATES · MEXICO

CHIAPANECAS

Ladies of Chiapas

CD 7:8

Mexican Folk Song
English Version by MMH

A

do

Spanish: Cuan - do la no - che lle - gó, (clap clap)
English: Now that the night has ar - rived, (clap clap)

y con su man - to de a - zul (clap clap)
un - der a man - tle of blue, (clap clap)

El blan - co ran - cho cu - brió, (clap clap)
Un - der the moon shin - ing white, (clap clap)

a - le - gre el bai - le em - pe - zó. (clap clap)
I will go danc - ing with you. (clap clap)

128

Play △ on the 𝅗𝅥. in the B section.

Bai - la, mi chia - pa - ne - ca.
Dance, now, my *chia - pa - ne - ca.*

Bai - la, bai - la con gar - bo.
Dance with grace and en - chant - ment.

1.
Bai - la, sua - ve ra - yo de
Dance, now, with the moon___ shin - ing

luz._____
bright._____

2.
que en el bai - le rei - na e - res
Dance, my gen - tle one,___ You will

tú, chia - pa - ne - ca gen - til. (clap clap)
soon be the queen of the dance! (clap clap)

Reading a New Pitch: *Re*

CONCEPT
MELODY
SKILLS
SING, PLAY, DESCRIBE
LINKS
SCIENCE, LANGUAGE ARTS

This woman owns a pretty pig. Find the "oinks" in the song. Move to show the shape of the "oinks" patterns. On what pitch is the last "oink"? The pitch one step higher than *do* is **re**.

OLD WOMAN AND THE PIG

CD 7:12

American Folk Song

1. There was an old wom-an and she had a lit-tle pig,— Oink, oink, oink.
2. This lit-tle old wom-an kept the pig— in the barn,— Oink, oink, oink.

There was an old wom-an and she had a lit-tle pig,
This lit-tle old wom-an kept the pig— in the barn,

He did-n't cost much 'cause he was-n't ver-y big,— Oink, oink, oink.
The pret-ti-est thing she— had— on the farm,—Oink, oink, oink.

Here is the hand sign for *re*:

re

Sing the song. Use pitch-syllable
names and hand signs instead of the "oinks."

Sing the song again and **play** the "oinks."

Oink, oink, oink.

Practice with *Do Re Mi*

This bucket has a hole in it. Listen as two people try to fix it. **Find** *do re mi* in this song.

There's a Hole in the Bucket

CD 7:15

American Dialogue Song
Traditional German Melody "Liebe Heinrich"

1. There's a hole in the buck-et, dear Li-za, dear Li-za,
2. Mend the hole, then, dear Geor-gie, dear Geor-gie, dear Geor-gie,
3. With__ what shall I mend it, dear Li-za, dear Li-za,
4. With a straw,__ dear Geor-gie, dear Geor-gie, dear Geor-gie,
5. The__ straw is too long,__ dear Li-za, dear Li-za,

There's a hole in the buck-et, dear Li-za, a hole.
Mend the hole, then, dear Geor-gie, dear Geor-gie, the hole.
With__ what shall I mend it, dear Li-za, with what?
With a straw,__ dear Geor-gie, dear Geor-gie, a straw.
The__ straw is too long,__ dear Li-za, too long.

Liza:

6. Cut the straw, dear Georgie,
   dear Georgie, dear Georgie,
   Cut the straw, dear Georgie,
   dear Georgie, the straw.

8. With a knife, dear Georgie,
   ... a knife.

10. Then sharpen it, dear Georgie,
    ... then sharpen it.

Georgie:

7. With what shall I cut it,
   dear Liza, dear Liza,
   With what shall I cut it,
   dear Liza, with what?

9. The knife is too dull,
   dear Liza, ... too dull.

11. With what shall I sharpen it,
    dear Liza, ... with what?

132

Sing these two melodies. Use pitch syllables and hand signs.

a.

b.

Listen to a funny version of "Old MacDonald Had a Farm." Which of the melodies above do you hear on "E-I-E-I-O"? What animals do you think the instruments sound like?

LISTENING CD 7:18

Old MacDonald Had a Farm
arranged by Leroy Anderson

12. With a stone, dear Georgie,
    ... a stone.

13. The stone is too dry,
    dear Liza, ... too dry.

14. Then wet it, dear Georgie,
    ... then wet it.

15. With what shall I wet it,
    dear Liza, ... with what?

16. With water, dear Georgie,
    ... with water.

17. In what shall I get it,
    dear Liza, ... in what?

18. In a bucket, dear Georgie,
    ... in a bucket.

CONCEPT
RHYTHM

SKILLS
READ, PLAY, LISTEN

LINKS
SCIENCE, READING

Have you ever flown a kite? **Find** the dotted half notes in this kite song.

Let's Go Fly a Kite

from the movie *Mary Poppins*

CD 7:19

Verse

Words and Music by Richard M. Sherman and Robert B. Sherman

1. With____ tup-pence for pa - per and strings,
2. When you send____ it fly - ing up there,

You can have your own set of wings;
All at once you're light - er than air;

With your feet on the ground you're a bird in flight
You can dance on the breeze o - ver hous - es and trees

With your fist hold - ing tight
With your fist hold - ing tight

to the string of your kite. Oh!____
to the string of your kite. Oh!____

Read this pattern.

Sing the song and **play** this pattern on the Refrain.

Refrain

Let's go fly a kite, Up to the high - est height! Let's go fly a kite, And send it soar - ing, Up through the at - mos - phere, Up where the air is clear. Oh, let's go fly a kite!

135

Listen and Play with the Wind

Can you see wind? **Listen** to this windy music. It is an étude. An *étude* is music that is written to help piano students build playing skill and strength.

MIDI

Use MIDIsaurus CD-ROM to practice ♩.

LISTENING CD 7:22

Étude Op. 25, No. 11, "The Winter Wind"
by Frédéric Chopin

Meet the Musician

Frédéric Chopin started learning the piano at the age of four. He gave his first concerts at the age of eight. He began writing piano music in his teens. He left his home in Poland to perform and write music all over Europe.

THINK! Why do you think this music is known as "The Winter Wind Étude"?

Speak this poem about the wind.

Who Has Seen the Wind?

Who has seen the wind?
   Neither I nor you:
But when the leaves hang trembling
   The wind is passing thro'.

Who has seen the wind?
   Neither you nor I:
But when the trees bow down their heads
   The wind is passing by.

Christina Georgina Rossetti

Play this pattern as you speak the poem.
Play any pitches from C D E G A in any order.

Bells/Orff Instruments

What other sounds or movement can you
add to show the wind?
Form small groups to read, play, and act
out a verse of the poem.

CONCEPT
MELODY

SKILLS
LISTEN, READ,
IMPROVISE

LINKS
CULTURES,
SCIENCE

Listen to music that you might hear at a street fair in New York City.

 LISTENING CD 7:23

Somos Boricuas (We Are Puerto Rican)
by Juan Gutiérrez

Someone who repairs shoes is called a cobbler. *Zapatero* is Spanish for cobbler.
Read this song using pitch syllables and hand signs.
Form two groups and take turns singing this song.

MAP

UNITED STATES ← PUERTO RICO

EL ZAPATERO

The Cobbler

CD 7:24

Puerto Rican Folk Song

Cobbler

Spanish: Mis ni - ñi - tos, ¿a dón - de van us - te - des?
English: Ni - ño, Ni - ña, wher - ev - er are you go - ing?

Group

Za - pa - te - ro, nos va - mos a pa - sear.
Cob - bler, cob - bler, we're go - ing for a stroll.

Cobbler

Mis ni-ñi-tos, los za-pa-tos se rom-pen.
Ni-ño, Ni-ña, you'll wear your shoes out walk-ing.

Group

Za-pa-te-ro, us-ted los com-pon-drá.
Cob-bler, cob-bler, then will you mend the hole?

Reading *Re* in Wales

You are learning to read *re*. Let's see how much you remember.

1 What pitches is *re* between?

2 If *do* is in the first space, where is *re*?

3 If *do* is around the first line, where is *re*?

"Shoheen Sho" is a lullaby from Wales. **Read** this song with pitch syllables. Then **sing** it with the words.

MAP

WALES

UNITED STATES

shoheen sho

CD 7:28

Welsh Folk Song
Verse 1 Traditional Welsh Words
Verses 2 and 3 by Margaret Campbelle-duGard

do

1. Sho - heen sho, ba - by boy,
   Bird - ie sleeps in the nest,

Fa - ther's pride, Moth - er's joy.
Sun doth sink in the West.

2. Shoheen sho, baby girl,
   Father's pride, Mother's pearl.
   Birdie sleeps in the nest,
   Sun doth sink in the West.

3. Shoheen sho, little dove,
   Fill my heart full of love.
   Birdie sleeps in the nest,
   Sun doth sink in the West.

Learn About Wales

Wales is known for its mountains, its castles, its rugby, and its singing.

Some of the greatest opera singers, such as Bryn Terfel, are proud to be Welsh.

Welsh choirs are famous all over the world.

Welsh boys playing rugby

Listen to the Welsh National anthem sung by Welsh men's choirs.

LISTENING CD 7:31

**Hen wlad fy nhadau
(The Land of my Fathers)**
Morriston Orpheus Choir and the Welsh Guards

Morriston Orpheus Choir at Carnegie Hall, New York

Harlech Castle in Wales, Great Britain

141

CONCEPT
RHYTHM
SKILLS
DESCRIBE,
PLAY, LISTEN
LINKS
HISTORY, FINE
ART, DANCE

A hat with three corners is called a *tricorn* hat. Tricorn hats were worn more than 200 years ago. Because of their shape, they would not blow off your head easily. This was useful since many people rode horses at that time.

Mein Hut

My Hat

CD 7:32

German Folk Song

German: **Mein Hut** er hat drei Eck - en,
English: **My hat** it has three cor - ners,

Drei Eck - en hat mein Hut,
Three cor - ners has my hat,

Und hätt er nicht drei Eck - en,
And had it not three cor - ners,

Dann ist er nicht mein Hut.
It would er not be my hat.

Move as you sing the song. Leave out one action word on each repeat.

My

hat

three

corners

Play this pattern as you sing the song.

Bells/Orff Instruments

Move and Play with a Minuet

The minuet was a dance popular in the late 1700s. *Minuet* means "little steps."

Art Gallery

Minuet **by Giovanni Domenico Tiepolo**

Giovanni Domenico Tiepolo was an Italian painter during the 1700s. His father was a great painter and his teacher as well

Play each pattern lightly. Find these patterns in the listening map.

Learn some minuet steps with a partner.
Play the patterns and move with minuet steps.

144

This minuet is music from a play.

LISTENING CD 8:1

Minuet from *Abdelazar*

by Henry Purcell

Follow the listening map. **Listen** for the different brass instruments taking turns on the melody.

Listening Map for Minuet

This minuet is in ABBAB form. The B section does not repeat the second time through.

CONCEPT
MELODY
SKILLS
READ, CREATE, PLAY
LINKS
SOCIAL STUDIES

Board the boat!

Many years ago people traveled to America by boat. This song is about people boarding the boat.

Find *do* in this song. **Read** the song with pitch syllables.

Sammy Sackett

CD 8:2

American Folk Song

do

Sam - my Sack - ett, hold on to my jack - et,

Hold on to my coat. That's the way we board the boat.

Sing the song and play the game for "Sammy Sackett." When the leader taps you, everyone sings your name instead of "Sammy."

Find these patterns in "Sammy Sackett." Create a new melody by putting the patterns in order. Play and sing your melody.

Question and Answer

When you ask a question, someone gives an answer. In music there are questions and answers, too.

The question ends "up in the air." It does not end on *do*. The answer has a "final" feeling because it ends on *do*.

Read this melody.

Bells/Orff Instruments

THINK! Why does the melody above sounds like a musical question?

Play the question.

Create an answer by ending on *do*. Change only the last three notes.

Listen for a melody that sounds like the one you just played. Raise your hand when you hear it. This music is played by the U.S. Marine Drum and Bugle Corps.

 LISTENING CD 8:5

We're Looking Good
by John Williams

U.S. Marine Drum and Bugle Corps ▲

▼ **Philippine Marine Drum and Bugle Team performing in Makati City, Philippines**

149

LESSON
7

CONCEPT
STYLE
SKILLS
SING, DESCRIBE, LISTEN
LINKS
SCIENCE, FINE ART

The rabbit in this song has mighty long ears. What do you notice about the verses of the song? Form two groups and **sing** the song.

Mister Rabbit, Mister Rabbit

CD 8:6

Southern Folk Song

Verse

Friend

1. Mis-ter Rab-bit, Mis-ter Rab-bit, your ears' might-y long!
2. Mis-ter Rab-bit, Mis-ter Rab-bit, your coat's might-y gray!
3. Mis-ter Rab-bit, Mis-ter Rab-bit, your tail's might-y white!

Rabbit

Yes in - deed, they're put on wrong._
Yes in - deed, 'twas made that way.___
Yes in - deed, I'm go-ing out of sight.__

Refrain

All

Ev' - ry lit - tle soul must shine, shine, shine._

Ev' - ry lit - tle soul must shine,_ shine, shine.

Young Hare
by Albrecht Dürer

A **folk song** is a song by an unknown composer. It has been passed on from one person to another for many years.

Find where the music tells you that "Mister Rabbit, Mister Rabbit" is a folk song.

Can you find other folk songs in this book?

Use **music.mmhschool.com** to research folk songs on the web.

Going to the Opera

This music is from an opera. An **opera** is a story told through music.

A solo by a singer in an opera is called an *aria*. Music with two people singing is called a *duet*. Sometimes the two singers take turns. Sometimes they both sing at the same time.

LISTENING CD 8:9

Papagena! Papagena! Papagena! from *The Magic Flute* by Wolfgang Amadeus Mozart

Listen to the duet between Papageno and Papagena. It is from the opera *The Magic Flute*. Hold up your right hand when you hear Papageno, the man. Hold up your left hand when you hear Papagena, the woman.

Papageno and Papagena in *The Magic Flute* ▶

Opera has singing, acting, scenery, costumes, and sometimes dancing.

Wolfgang Amadeus Mozart was from Austria. He began to play the harpsichord, which is an early keyboard instrument, when he was 3 years old. By the age of 6, he was composing his own music. When he was 11, his first opera was performed.

THINK! How are "Mister Rabbit, Mister Rabbit" and "Papagena! Papagena! Papagena!" from *The Magic Flute* alike?

153

Read and Play *Do, Re, Mi,* and *So*

CONCEPT
MELODY
SKILLS
READ, LISTEN,
PLAY
LINKS
CULTURES,
SOCIAL STUDIES,
FINE ART

This song is a Native American lullaby from the Muscogee Creek Nation of Oklahoma. It is about a mother who has gone to hunt for turtles.

Read the song using pitch syllables and hand signs. **Sing** the song.

CD 8:10

Muskogee Creek Lullaby
As Sung by Lillian Rainer

Creek: Ba - by No - dja

No - dja No - dja

la - dja ho - ho gan ai - yang - si

ma - ki - to wa - la - ka - his

ma - ki - to ai - yang - si

Ba - by No - dja

Taos Village is in northern New Mexico. It has been the home of the Taos Native Americans for more than 800 years.

This round dance is performed by the Taos people. Form a circle and step with the beat as you listen.

 LISTENING / CD 8:12

Taos Round Dance (Traditional)

The village where the Taos people live is called a *pueblo. Pueblo* is the Spanish word for "town."

A pueblo is made up of houses with many floors around a central square. The houses are made of adobe, which is a brick made of mud and straw.

Art Gallery

Taos July by Joseph Amadeus Fleck

Adobe buildings in Taos Pueblo, New Mexico

155

Take Turns Playing

Name some ways you can take turns in music.

You'll Sing a Song and I'll Sing a Song

CD 8:13

Words and Music by Ella Jenkins

You'll sing a song, and I'll sing a song,

and we'll sing a song to - geth - er.

You'll sing a song, and I'll sing a song,

in warm or win - try weath - er.

Meet the Musician

Ella Jenkins grew up in Chicago. She performs with and teaches children around the world. She has been to all seven continents including Antarctica. Much of the music she writes helps us to get to know people from other countries. Ella was awarded the "Grammy 2004 Lifetime Achievement Award" for her work in music.

Listen as Ella speaks about writing songs.

RECORDED INTERVIEW CD 8:16

Sing the song again. **Play** this bell part with the song.

Bells/Orff Instruments
Play 3 times

Ella Jenkins with students from ▼
Middleton Elementary School;
Skokie, Illinois

Spotlight Your Success!

REVIEW

1 How many beats does a dotted half note last for in $\frac{3}{4}$?

    a. 1   **b.** 2   **c.** 3   **d.** 4

2 Which is the hand sign for *re*?

    a.   **b.**

READ AND LISTEN

Read these patterns. Then **listen**. Which do you hear?

1 Which pattern has only *do, re,* and *mi*?

    a.

    b.

2 Which rhythm pattern has a dotted half note?

    a.

    b.

THINK!

1. Which of these songs are folk songs? How do you know?

   Hello, Hello, There
   Chiapanecas
   Old Woman and the Pig

2. **Write** about a song or listening you like. Tell why you like it.

CREATE AND PERFORM

Question:

Answer:

1. **Read** and clap the rhythms for the question and the answer with a partner.

2. **Create** a melody using *do, re, mi,* and *so* for each part. End the question on *so.* End the answer on *do.*

3. **Perform** your question and answer, taking turns.

Meet the Musician
ON NATIONAL RADIO!

Name: Trevor Ochieng
Age: 14
Instrument: Violin
Home Town: Wyandanch, New York

Trevor Ochieng was only three years old the first time he played the violin onstage. He remembers feeling scared. "My teacher brought me onto the stage, but once she left, I was too nervous to start playing," he says.

Trevor's teacher decided to stand next to him to help him feel better. Trevor began to play his violin, but when his teacher tried to leave the stage again, Trevor stopped and tried to follow her. Again and again his teacher tried to walk offstage, but Trevor would only play when she stood nearby. "My teacher had to stay right by my side the whole time!" says Trevor.

Since then, Trevor has performed onstage many times. Luckily, he doesn't get "stage fright" anymore!

LISTENING CD 8:18–19 **RECORDED INTERVIEW**

Scherzo and Tarantella by Henryk Wieniawski

Listen to Trevor's performance and interview on the national radio program **From the Top**.

Spotlight on the Clarinet

Did You Know?

The clarinet's inventor thought its high notes sounded like a trumpet or "clarino," so he named it after that instrument.

The clarinet is a single-reed instrument. Sound is produced when the player blows across a thin strip of wood, called a *reed*, to make it vibrate.

The clarinet's body is made up of five separate pieces that fit together.

The clarinet has changed little since it was invented, about 300 years ago.

 LISTENING CD 8:20–21

Peter and the Wolf by Sergei Prokofiev

Dance Preludes for Clarinet and Piano, No. 3 by Witold Lutoslawski

Listen to these pieces for clarinet. The Prokofiev clarinet part is heard when the cat appears in the story of "Peter and the Wolf." In the piece by Lutoslawski, you can hear the very high, brilliant sound of the clarinet.

UNIT 5

The Music in Us!

You will find many ways that people make music in this unit. Maybe you will find some new ways to make music yourself!

Coming Attractions

Play pentatonic with a donkey.

Help an elephant find its trunk in $\frac{2}{4}$.

Listen and ride a motorcycle with a trombone.

You can make music, even if you are not a virtuoso. A *virtuoso* is a very good musician.

Sing a song about how we all have music inside us.

Everybody Has Music Inside

CD 8:22

Swing (♫ = ♪♩)

Words and Music by Greg Scelsa

Ev-'ry-bod-y has mu-sic in - side___ es - pe-cial-ly for you.

Don't be a - fraid___ to let it out,___ it is-n't hard to do.___

You don't have to be a vir - tu - o - so,

it does - n't mat - ter if you sing just "so - so."

It's a feel-ing down in-side your soul, so come on, you can do___ it!

Ev-'ry-bod-y has mu-sic in - side,___ so let a song ring out.___

Just let it come right from your heart,

that's what it's all a - bout.

Mu - sic is the sound of life

reach-ing out for love.

Ev - 'ry-bod - y has mu - sic,

Ev - 'ry - bod - y has mu - sic,

Ev - 'ry-bod - y has mu - sic in - side.

Read these patterns. Which pattern goes with the verse and which goes with the refrain?

1 barn   barn   dance in the   barn

2 barn   barn   in the   barn

In $\frac{2}{\text{.}}$ meter there are two beats to a measure. The **dotted quarter note** gets the beat in this meter.

A dot after a note makes the note longer. The ♩. is as long as three eighth notes ♪♪♪

Here are the patterns you clapped above.

Refrain

Verse

Play the patterns with the song.

Move and Play with Elephants

tuba

This $\frac{2}{4}$ music is about an elephant named Effie who goes folk dancing! The solo instrument is the lowest-pitched brass instrument, called the *tuba*.

Gradually getting slower in music is called **ritardando**. Gradually getting faster is called **accelerando**.

Listen for the tuba in the music. **Move** like an elephant with the beat. Watch out for the *ritardando* and the *accelerando*!

 LISTENING CD 8:28

Effie Goes Folk Dancing by Alec Wilder

168

Read this poem in $\frac{2}{\text{(dotted half note)}}$ meter.

The Elephant Carries a Great Big Trunk

The elephant carries a great big trunk;
He never packs it with clothes;
It has no lock and it has no key,
But he takes it wherever he goes.

Anonymous

Sometimes the same word can mean two things.
What trunk is the poem talking about?

Read this pattern. Play the pattern with the poem:

Playalong

Dance,   El - e -phant,   El - e -phant, dance!

Play the pattern with "Effie Goes Folk Dancing."

LESSON 2

CONCEPT
MELODY
SKILLS
SING, READ, PLAY
LINKS
FINE ART, READING

Discover Pentatonic Scales

Pull up the anchor and set sail on this ship.
Sing the *response* after the captain *calls*.

CD 8:29

American Sea Chantey

Verse
Call

do

1. Oh, the an-chor is weighed and the sails they are set,
2. We've a jol-ly good ship and a jol-ly good crew,
3. Oh,— say, were you ev-er in Ri — o Grande?

Response

A - way————— for Ri - o!

Call

The friends that we're leav-ing we'll nev-er for-get,
A jol-ly good mate and a good skip-per too,
It's there that the riv-ers run down gold-en sand,

Response

For we're bound for Ri - o Grande!

U.S.S. Constitution

by Myron Clark

The U.S.S. Constitution was a ship that was made of wood. The wooden sides were so thick that in a battle in 1812, the cannon balls bounced off. The ship then became known as "Old Ironsides."

The pitches in the crew's responses are *do re mi so* and *la*.

When these five pitches are placed in order, they create a scale. A five-tone scale is called **pentatonic**.

Sing the responses of the song. Use pitch syllables and hand signs.

Refrain
All

And a - way___ for Ri-o! Aye___ for Ri-o!

So fare ye well,___ my bon - ny young friend,

We are bound for Ri - o Grande!

Sing and Play in Pentatonic

Cookie and his friend are talking. Find out what is missing. Pick a part and **sing** the song.

CD 8:32

Freely

Calypso Song from the West Indies

Verse

Friend

Cookie

"Cook-ie____ are you sure no-bo-dy passed here?" "No, my friend."

Friend

Cookie

"Cook-ie____ are you sure no-bo-dy passed here?" "No, my friend."

Refrain

Friend

Cookie

"Well, {one / two} of my dump-lin's gone." "Don't tell____ me so!"

Friend

Cookie

{"One / "Two} of my dump-lin's gone." "Don't tell____ me so!"

Friend

{"One / "Two} of my dump-lin's gone."

Describe what happens in the song.

What five pitches are used
in the verse?

Cookie   Friend

do   re   mi   so   la

D   E   F#   A   B

Choose a partner. **Play**
with the verse of the song.

CONCEPT
RHYTHM

SKILLS
LISTEN,
SING, READ

LINKS
CULTURES,
FINE ART

Global Voices

MAP

UNITED STATES   CYPRUS

Cyprus is an island near Turkey. Look at the pictures of Cyprus. Compare it with the place you live. How is it the same? How is it different?

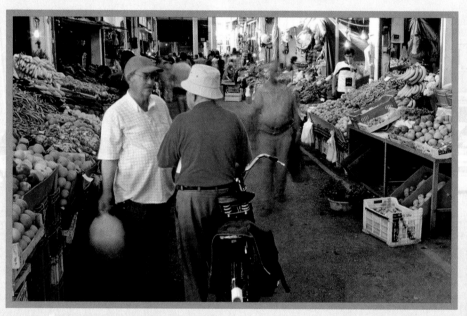

Cyprus is known for its olives, wine, and fruit. It is also known for beautiful artwork, such as pottery, baskets, and weaving.

Art Gallery

Pilgrim Flask

This piece of pottery is from Cyprus. It was made many years ago.

Listen to this song from Cyprus in $\frac{2}{\cdot}$.

POUN TO, POUN TO

🔘 CD 9:1

Where Is It? Where Is It?
Greek & Cypriot Children's game song

Πού 'ν' το, πού 'ν' το, το δακτυλίδι
Ψάξε, ψάξε, δεν θα το βρεις.
Δεν θα το βρεις, δεν θα το βρεις,
Το δακτυλίδι πον ζητείζ.

Where is it, where is (it), the ring
Look for it, look for it, you will not find it.
You will not find it, you will not find it
The ring that you are looking (asking) for.

In $\frac{2}{\cdot}$ meter you will often find this rhythm: ♩♪

poun to poun to

Listen to the song. Identify the words in the song that have this rhythm. **Clap** the rhythm as you sing it.

175

Read a Song in ²⁄

Who is wearing buttons today? Tell what the meter is of this song. **Read** and clap the rhythm.

Button, You Must Wander

CD 9:2

American Singing Game

do

But - ton, you must wan - der, wan - der, wan - der,

But - ton, you must wan - der ev' - ry - where.

Bright eyes will find you, sharp eyes will find you.

But - ton, you must wan - der ev' - ry - where.

Sing the song and play the game.

MIDI

For another activity with "Button, You Must Wander," see *Spotlight on MIDI*.

176

This music has four French horns in it. The French horn is a member of the brass family.

"Pass" the beat as you **listen**. Gallop and then walk with the music. Which fits best? Is this music in $\frac{2}{}$ or $\frac{2}{}$?

LISTENING CD 9:5

La Choisy by Michel Corrette

THINK!

"Poun to, Poun to" and La Choisy are both in $\frac{2}{}$ meter and use similar rhythms. How are they different?

Read and Play Pentatonic

CONCEPT
MELODY
SKILLS
LISTEN, READ,
IMPROVISE
LINKS
CULTURES,
READING

Zydeco is a kind of folk music found in southern Louisiana. It often uses pentatonic melodies. **Play** rhythm instruments with the beat as you listen.

 LISTENING CD 9:6

Bon Chien by Clifton Chenier

Some people work on shrimp boats along the coast of Louisiana. When the boats come in from the sea, people like to go to the dock to meet them.

Listen to this song about going to meet the shrimp boats.

LISTENING CD 9:7

Shrimp Boats by Paul Howard and Paul Weston

zydeco band ▼

Which lines in this song are alike?
Identify pitches in lines 3 and 4. **Read**
them with pitch syllables and hand signs.

CD 9:8

Words and Music by
Paul Howard and Paul Weston

Shrimp boats is a - com - in', their sails are in sight.

Shrimp boats is a - com - in', there's danc - in' to - night.

Why don't you hur – ry, hur – ry, hur – ry home?

Why don't you hur – ry, hur – ry, hur – ry home!

Shrimp boats is a - com - in', there's danc - in' to - night.

A Song in Pentatonic

This little donkey is not feeling well. Can you help him? How many pitches are in this song?

El burrito enfermo

The Sick Little Donkey

CD 9:11

Latin American Folk Song
Arranged by José-Luis Orozco
English Words by Linda Worsley

Spanish: A mi bu - rro, a mi bu - rro
English: Lit - tle don - key, my don - key,

le due - le la ca - be - za,
my don - key has a head - ache.

y el mé - di - co le man - da
The doc - tor came and gave him

[Cumulative: for each new verse, add previous line]

u - na go - rri - ta ne - gra, [u - na go - rri - ta ne - gra]
a black cap for his head - ache, [a black cap for his head - ache.]

y mue - ve las pa - ti - tas (tap, tap, tap, tap).
And now his lit - tle hooves go (tap, tap, tap, tap).

180

Read this bell part. Use pitch syllables and hand signs.

Play the bell part as you sing the song.

2. A mi burro, a mi burro
   le duele la garganta,
   y el médico le manda
   una bufanda blanca,
   una bufanda blanca,
   una gorrita negra
   y mueve las patitas
   (tap, tap, tap, tap).

3. A mi burro, a mi burro
   ya no le duele nada,
   y el médico le manda
   trocitos de manzana,
   trocitos de manzana,
   una bufanda blanca,
   una gorrita negra
   y mueve las patitas
   (tap, tap, tap, tap).

Little donkey, my donkey,
my donkey has a sore throat.
The doctor came and gave him
a white scarf for his sore throat,
a white scarf for his sore throat,
a black cap for his headache.
And now his little hooves go
(tap, tap, tap, tap).

Little donkey, my donkey,
my donkey's feeling better.
The doctor came and gave him
some little bits of apple,
some little bits of apple,
a white scarf for his sore throat,
a black cap for his headache.
And now his little hooves go
(tap, tap, tap, tap).

Learn and Play Orff Instruments

CONCEPT
TONE COLOR
SKILLS
DESCRIBE, LISTEN, PLAY
LINKS
CULTURES, FINE ART

There are three kinds of Orff instruments. Each is made from a different material, so it has a different sound.

Carl Orff designed them. He wanted them to represent sounds from different parts of the world. He chose the xylophone from Africa. The metallophone came from Indonesia. He chose the glockenspiel from his own country, Austria. Look at the pictures and name the three types of Orff instruments.

Orff alto xylophone   Orff alto metallophone   Orff alto glockenspiel

xylophone   gamelan metallophone   glockenspiel

Speak this to learn the names of Orff instruments.

CD 9:18

Orff Instruments

By Donna Otto and Janet Graham

A

Orff in - stru - ments! Orff in - stru - ments!

Learn a - bout each name, Then you can play a game!

B

Xy - lo - phones have wood-en bars, wood-en bars, wood-en bars,

Xy - lo - phones have wood-en bars, Rose - wood bars.

C

Met - al - lo - phones have met - al bars, met - al bars, met - al bars,

Met - al - lo - phones have met - al bars, Gray met - al bars.

D

Glock - en - spiels have ti - ny bars, ti - ny bars, shi - ny bars,

Go back to **A** *and repeat.*

Glock - en - spiels have ti - ny bars, ti - ny, shi - ny bars.

Play with a Lullaby

A lullaby is soft music that can help you fall asleep. A *berceuse* is a kind of lullaby.

Listen to this berceuse. **Pat** the beat as you listen to feel the $\frac{2}{\cdot}$ meter.

 LISTENING CD 9:21

Berceuse by Gunild Keetman

Meet the Musician

Gunild Keetman was a dancer and composer. She worked with Carl Orff. She enjoyed teaching music to children. Her knowledge of dance helped her find ways to use movement to learn.

Gunild Keetman with students ▼

Choose an instrument. **Play** this pattern softly with "Berceuse."

Playalong

What are things to think about when choosing an instrument to play with this music?

Art Gallery

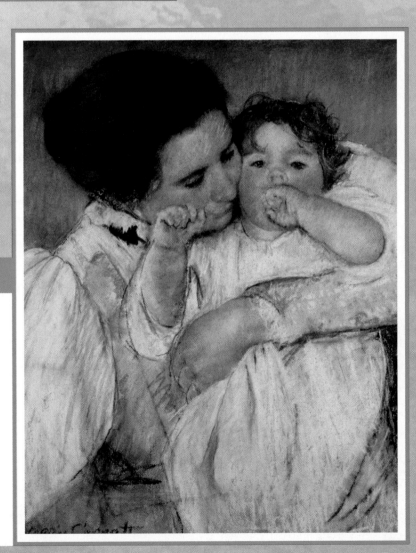

Mother and Child
by Mary Cassatt

Mary Cassatt loved to paint mothers and children. Born in Pennsylvania, she studied painting in Europe. She became one of the most important American painters of her time.

CONCEPT
MELODY
SKILLS
READ, IMPROVISE,
PLAY
LINKS
CULTURES

The frog in this song is from China. **Read** the first line of the song. Use pitch syllables and hand signs.

MAP

UNITED STATES → CHINA

I Chih Ching Wa

Frogs

CD 9:22

Chinese Folk Song
English Words by Linda Worsley

Chinese: 一 只 青 蛙 一 张 嘴 两 只 眼 睛 四 条 腿
English: Frog-gy has one mouth, you see. And two eyes, four legs has he.

乒 乓 乒 乓 跳 下 水 呀 青 蛙 不 吃 水
pin pong pin pong Jump down, frog. The Frog-gy will not drink,

太 平 年 青 蛙 不 吃 水 太 平 年
When it's calm, Frog-gy will not drink. When it's calm,

青 蛙 向 水 里 跳 洗 个 痛 快 的 澡。
he will take a bath. Frog jumped in! Have a hap-py bath, Mis-ter Frog!

Improvise a melody to go with this frog poem. Use pentatonic pitches.

Do you want my little frog?
Could you please house and feed him?
It isn't that he isn't nice.
I guess I just don't need him!

Hazel Copeland

The instruments are from China.
Do they look like any you know?

CD-ROM

Use *World Instruments* CD-ROM to learn more about instruments in China.

yangquin ▶

◀ dizi

gu ▶

Play a Descant

Have you ever seen a wolf put his socks on? Name the actions of the wolf in this song. Practice the actions while speaking the Spanish words. **Sing** the song.

Jugaremos en el bosque
We Will Play in the Forest

CD 9:26

Collected and Transcribed by Carol J. Brown
English Words by Linda Worsley

Spanish: Ju - ga - re - mos en el bos - que mien - tras que el lo - bo no es - tá.

English: We'll be play - ing in the for - est when the wolf is no - where near.

Y si el lo - bo a - pa - re - ce a to - dos nos co - me - rá.

If he comes back to the for - est, he will get us all, I fear.

(Wolf answers)

Spoken: ¿Lo - bo, lo - bi - to es - tás a - llí?

Wolf, won't you tell us, are you there?

Wolf answers:

1. Me estoy bañando.

2. Me estoy secando.

3. Me estoy peinando.

4. Me estoy poniendo los tenis.

5. ¡Alli voy!

1. I'm taking a bath.

2. I'm drying off.

3. I'm combing my hair.

4. I'm putting on my tennis shoes.

5. I'm coming!

188

A *descant* is a higher part that goes along with a melody. Name the pitches in this descant. **Play** the descant with the song.

Part 1

Part 2

189

CONCEPT
INSTRUMENTAL
TONE COLOR

SKILLS
SING, LISTEN,
DESCRIBE

LINKS
HISTORY

Dela is wearing something special
in this song. What is it?

What Did Delaware?

CD 9:32

American Folk Song

1. What did Del - a - ware? Oh, what did Del - a - ware?
   wore her New Jer - sey. She wore her New Jer - sey. She

What did Del - a - ware? Oh, what did Del - a - ware?
wore her New Jer - sey. She wore her New Jer - sey. She

What did Del - a - ware? Oh, what did Del - a - ware? I
wore her New Jer - sey. She wore her New Jer - sey. I

ask you as a friend of mine. What did Del - a - ware? She
tell you as a friend of mine. She wore her New Jer - sey.

2. Why did Caliphone ya?   She phoned to say "Hawaya."
   Why did Caliphone? . . .   Phoned to say "Hawaya." . . .
   I ask you as a friend of mine, I tell you as a friend of mine.
   Why did Caliphone?   She phoned to say "Hawaya."

To slide up or down very fast in music is called *glissando*.

Listen for glissandos in this music. Pretend you are playing a trombone as you listen.

🔘 **LISTENING** ⟩ CD 10:1

Lassus Trombone by Henry Fillmore

Meet the Musician

Henry Fillmore was a composer from Cincinnati, Ohio. He wrote a lot of band music. He liked the slide trombone. He even played it with a circus at one time.

Dixieland band ▼

Learn About Dixieland Bands

Dixieland music is an early type of jazz. It started in the African American communities of New Orleans. Dixieland was played for parties, parades, weddings, and even funerals.

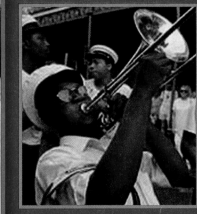

The musicians improvise, or make up, melodies and rhythms while they are playing. Most bands have a cornet, a clarinet, a trombone, a tuba, and drums. Other instruments such as a banjo, a saxophone, a string bass, and a piano are also often used.

191

Ride with a Trombone

mouthpiece ▶   ◀ slide

                                        ◀ bell

The trombone is a large brass instrument. Only the tuba sounds lower than the trombone.

Different pitches can be created by making the lips tighter or looser. Different pitches are also created by moving the slide to different positions.

You are about to hear the trombone in a concerto. First, **listen** to this music and learn how to ride!

LISTENING CD 10:2

Motorcycle Ride by Bruce Haack and Esther Nelson

Listen to hear what makes
this music unusual.

Use **Orchestral Instruments**
CD-ROM to learn more
about the trombone and
other brass instruments.

   CD 10:3

Motorbike Concerto
by Jan Sandström

Listen and follow the map.

Listening Map for *Motorbike Concerto*

Introduction:
Fasten your helmet!

Start-up!

Home again! Into
the garage! Whew!

Read and Move to *Do Re Mi So La*

CONCEPT
MELODY
SKILLS
READ, SING
LINKS
DANCE,
READING

What does it mean to "jim along"? Let's jim, tiptoe, jog, and jump along with this song.
Read the first four lines of this song. Use pitch syllables and hand signs.

Jim Along, Josie

CD 10:4

American Folk Song

do

1. Hey, jim a - long, jim a - long, Jo - sie,

Hey, jim a - long, jim a - long, Joe!

Hey, jim a - long, jim a - long, Jo - sie,

Hey, jim a - long, jim a - long, Joe!

Sing the song and move to it.

A Section ▼

B Section ▲

Read the poem. Then **compose** a melody for the poem using *do, re, mi, so,* and *la.* End the first two lines on *so* for the musical question. End the last two lines on *do* for the musical answer.

Happy Thoughts

The world is so full
  of a number of things,
I'm sure we should all be
  as happy as kings.

Robert Louis Stevenson

Ⓑ *(same words each time)*

Face to the cen - ter, hands on your knees,

Clap three times and turn a - round, please!

2. Tiptoe along, . . .

3. Jog, jog along, . . .

4. Jump, jump along, . . .

5. Do what you want, . . .

195

Sing with Pitch Syllables

Singing can brighten any day.

Sing! Sing! Sing!

CD 10:7

Music and Words by Branice McKenzie

Swing (♩♩ = ♩.♩)

Verse

do

1. I'm talk-ing to the trees and birds, things a-round the u-ni-verse.
2. I'm walk-ing, skip-ping, run-ning free, el-e-phants can talk to me.

Sing, Sing, Sing.___

{ Clouds and flow-ers rain-y days,
My heart and mind can al-ways see,

love them all___ just the same. } Sing, Sing, Sing.___
all the good things here in me.

{ When-
It

ev-er I am feel-ing low, I take my smile and go, go, go.
is-n't just a luck-y chance_ that the peo-ple want to dance.

Sing, Sing, Sing.___

{ Ne-ver will I be a-fraid,
Re-mem-ber can and ne-ver can't,

Sing the pitches for each *Sing, Sing, Sing* from the song. Are the pitches always the same each time? Sing the song. Use pitch syllables and hand signs for each *Sing, Sing, Sing.*

THINK! What is your favorite way of enjoying music? Why?

mu - sic I can al - ways make.
spread your wings and ne - ver land. } Sing, Sing, Sing.___

Refrain

Let's all just sing, make me mu - sic, make me hap - py.___

Let's all just sing, make me ma - gic.___ Sing, Sing, Sing.___

Spotlight Your Success!

REVIEW

1 Which pattern shows *do re mi so la*?

do

do

2 Which shows a pattern in 2/. meter?

a.

b.

READ AND LISTEN

Read these patterns, then **listen** to identify.

1 Which pattern is in 2/. meter?

a.

b.

2 Which pattern uses *do re mi so la*?

a.

b.

THINK!

1 If you composed a melody about a galloping pony, would you use $\frac{2}{4}$ or $\frac{2}{4}$ meter? Why? What brass instrument would you choose to play your melody about the pony? Why?

2 List the favorite music and songs in this unit. Create a class graph that shows how many chose each piece. **Write** about the favorite piece and why you think it was chosen.

CREATE AND PERFORM

In groups, **create** a performance of "The Elephant Carries a Great Big Trunk" with a narrator, movement, and instruments.

Tell: • Your choice of rhythms.
      • Your choice of instruments.
      • Things you did well and those that need work.

Perform your piece.

Meet the Musician
ON NATIONAL RADIO!

Name: Rebecca Brown
Age: 9
Instrument: Guitar
Home Town: Chicago, Illinois

Nine-year-old Rebecca Brown loves to practice her guitar. "I practice in the morning, after school, and before I go to bed," she says. "I play guitar if I'm happy or sad, frustrated or glad!"

Rebecca learns to play a song first by listening to it on a recording. Then she tries to play the song on her guitar. Rebecca's teacher works with her to correct any mistakes.

Playing guitar is Rebecca's favorite thing to do, but she also likes to read books and draw pictures. She has won her school's spelling bee two years in a row!

LISTENING CD 10:11–14 **RECORDED INTERVIEW**

Packington's Pound (Anonymous)
and **Allegro** by Mauro Giuliani

Listen to Rebecca's performance and interview on the national radio program **From the Top**.

"Singing together makes us reach deeply into our hearts and lets us know these feelings will stay there for our whole lives," explains Peter Yarrow.

Mr. Yarrow has been singing folk music for many years with his friends Paul Stookey and Mary Travers. In 1963 they sang "Blowin' in the Wind" at the Civil Rights March on Washington, D.C. They told the world that America's unfairness to African Americans had to end.

Today Mr. Yarrow works on "Project Respect," a program to help children grow up in a safe world without name-calling and mean-spirited teasing. The song "Don't Laugh at Me" is the program's anthem. It reminds people to care for and respect one another. Mr. Yarrow knows that songs of truth can make the world a more peaceful place.

Spotlight on the Bass Drum

Did You Know?

Drums have been around for more than 6,000 years.

The bass drum can sometimes be as large as the person playing it.

When a bass drum is played in an orchestra, it stands on its side on a rack. The player strikes the head with a large stick, or *beater*.

LISTENING CD 10:15–16

Batik by Linda Worsley

The Rite of Spring
by Igor Stravinsky

Listen for the bass drum. It is played softly in "Batik" except when new instruments are added. In "*The Rite of Spring*," eleven very loud sounds are played on the bass drum before a wild dance begins.

Everything Grows

You can grow
in many ways,
including playing,
listening, composing,
and singing music.

Coming Attractions

Sing in a moon boat in pentatonic.

Create a rondo with hand jive.

Step, skip, and leap with animals from a rain forest.

Everyone and everything grows.
Find things on the page that grow.
Find them in the song.

What is the form of the song?

Everything Grows

CD 10:17

Music by Raffi
Words by Raffi and D. Pike

Refrain

Ev - 'ry-thing grows and grows.___

Ba - bies do, an - i - mals too. Ev - 'ry-thing grows.

Ev - 'ry-thing grows and grows.___

(last time)
End

Sis - ters do, bro - thers_ too.__ Ev - 'ry-thing grows.

Verse

1. A blade of grass,— fin-gers and toes,—
2. Food on the farm,— fish in the sea,—

Hair on—— my head, a red, red rose.
Birds in—— the air, leaves on the tree.

Go back to the beginning and sing to the End.

Ev-'ry-thing grows, an-y-one knows_ that's_ how_ it goes.

Rhythm in the Seasons!

CONCEPT
RHYTHM
SKILLS
NOTATE, CREATE, SING
LINKS
SCIENCE, FINE ART

Fall, winter, spring, summer!
Which is your favorite season?

Sing about a seed's journey.
What is the meter of this song?

Seeds and Seasons

CD 10:20

Words and Music by Jim Walters

Verse

1. When a show - er breaks o - ver the mea - dow,
2. And the wa - ter will whis - per the se - cret,
3. Then a shoot will grow in - to the sun - shine,

And the thun - der is heard on the plain,
It is time for the seed - ling to grow.
Reach - ing up for the heat and the light.

Ev - 'ry seed that in win - ter was sleep - ing
Ti - ny roots will reach down to the wa - ter,
Through the stem it will lift up the wa - ter,

Will a - wak - en and swell in the rain.
Tak - ing life from the warm earth be - low.
So the leaves will grow stur - dy and bright.

Read this poem. Pick four vegetables from the poem and **write** their rhythms.

from LITTLE SEEDS

Little seeds we sow in spring,
growing while the robins sing,
give us carrots, peas and beans,
tomatoes, pumpkins, squash and greens.

Else Holmelund Minarik

Refrain

And the sea-son will cir-cle, will cir-cle a-round,

And the sea-son will cir-cle a-round.

4. And the leaves blow and dance in the summer,
   Growing hardy and strong in the sun,
   Using nutrients, sunlight, and water,
   To make food until summer is done.
   Refrain

5. In the summer there may come a blossom,
   Where the bees find the nectar they need,
   Never knowing they carry the pollen,
   So the blossom can make a new seed.
   Refrain

6. Then at last when the leaves begin changing,
   Then the seed will fall into the ground.
   It will sleep in the meadow all winter,
   To awake when the spring comes around.
   Refrain

A Gardening Song in ⅔

Have you ever eaten a tortilla? Tortillas are flat bread. They are served at most meals in Mexico. This song is about growing corn to make tortillas. **Read** the rhythm. Practice the actions in the song.

MAP

UNITED STATES

MEXICO

LA BELLA HORTELANA

The Beautiful Gardener

CD 10:23

Traditional Mexican Song
English Words by Linda Worsley

Verse

Spanish: Cuan - do siem - bra, la be - lla hor - te - la - na,
English: When she goes sow - ing, the beau - ti - ful farm - er,

cuan - do siem - bra, siem - bra a - sí.
When she goes sow - ing, she sows just like this.

A - sí siem - bra po - co a po - co,
She sows the seeds, lit - tle by lit - tle,

Cumulative

lue - go po - ne las ma - nos a - sí Siem - bra a - sí
then she holds both her hands just like this, Sow - ing like this.

208

Art Gallery

Peasants by Diego Rivera

Diego Rivera was an artist from Mexico. He painted many pictures that show life in Mexico. The men in this picture are farming.

Clap these rhythms.

Name vegetables that match each rhythm.
Create a two-beat rhythm pattern using two of these vegetables. Clap your pattern during the Refrain of the song.

End

Lue - go po - ne las ma - nos a - sí.
Then she holds both her hands just like this.

Refrain

La, la, la, la, la, la, la, la, la.

Go back to the beginning and sing to the End.

La, la, la, la, la, la, la, la, la.

2. Cuando riega ...
3. Cuando corta ...
4. Cuando muele ...
5. Cuando come ...

2. When she goes watering
3. When she goes reaping
4. When she is grinding
5. When she is eating

209

CONCEPT
MELODY
SKILLS
READ,
LISTEN
LINKS
SCIENCE, FINE
ART, READING

Almost everyone enjoys seeing flowers growing wild. Yellow buttercups bloom in the spring in many parts of North America.

Art Gallery

Ranunculus by Charles Belle

Charles Belle is a French artist who likes to paint things found in nature. Ranunculus is the name of a group of flowers. One type is the buttercup.

Read this song. Use pitch syllables and hand signs.

ALL AROUND THE BUTTERCUP

CD 11:1

American Folk Song

All a-round the but-ter-cup, One! Two! Three!

If you want an-oth-er friend. Just choose me!

Sing each part with pitch syllables.
Play both patterns as you sing the song.

This music is about a day on a farm. **Listen** and tell what you think is happening on the farm.

LISTENING CD 11:4

The Farm

by Eugene Zador

Tell a Story on *Do Re Mi So*

Read this poem about a loyal friend.
Who is the friend?

Bliss

Let me fetch sticks,
Let me fetch stones,
Throw me your bones,
Teach me your tricks.

When you go ride,
Let me go run,
You in the sun,
Me at your side;

When you go swim,
Let me go too
Both lost in blue
Up to the brim;

Let me do this,
Let me do that—
What you are at,
That is my bliss.

Eleanor Farjeon

What do you think the boy is
saying to the dog?

Art Gallery

A Boy and His Dog
by Norman Rockwell

Norman Rockwell is a well-known
American artist. He painted
scenes of everyday American life.

Read the pitches in this song. Who is Blue?

OLD BLUE

CD 11:5

Southern Mountain Song

1. I had a dog and his name was Blue,
2. Chased that___ pos-sum up a hol - low tree,
3. Caught that___ pos-sum up a hol - low tree,
4. Baked that___ pos - sum___ good and brown,

I had a dog and his name was Blue,
Chased that___ pos-sum up a hol - low tree,
Caught that___ pos-sum up a hol - low tree,
Baked that___ pos - sum___ good and brown,

I had a dog and his name was Blue, and I
Chased that___ pos-sum up a hol - low tree,_____
Caught that___ pos-sum up a hol - low tree,_____
Baked that___ pos - sum___ good and brown,_____

bet - cha five dol - lars he's a good dog, too.
Best___ hunt-in' dog___ you___ ev-er did see.
Best___ hunt-in' dog___ you___ ev-er did see.
Laid___ sweet po-ta - ters___ all a - round.

Here, Blue, you good dog, you.

213

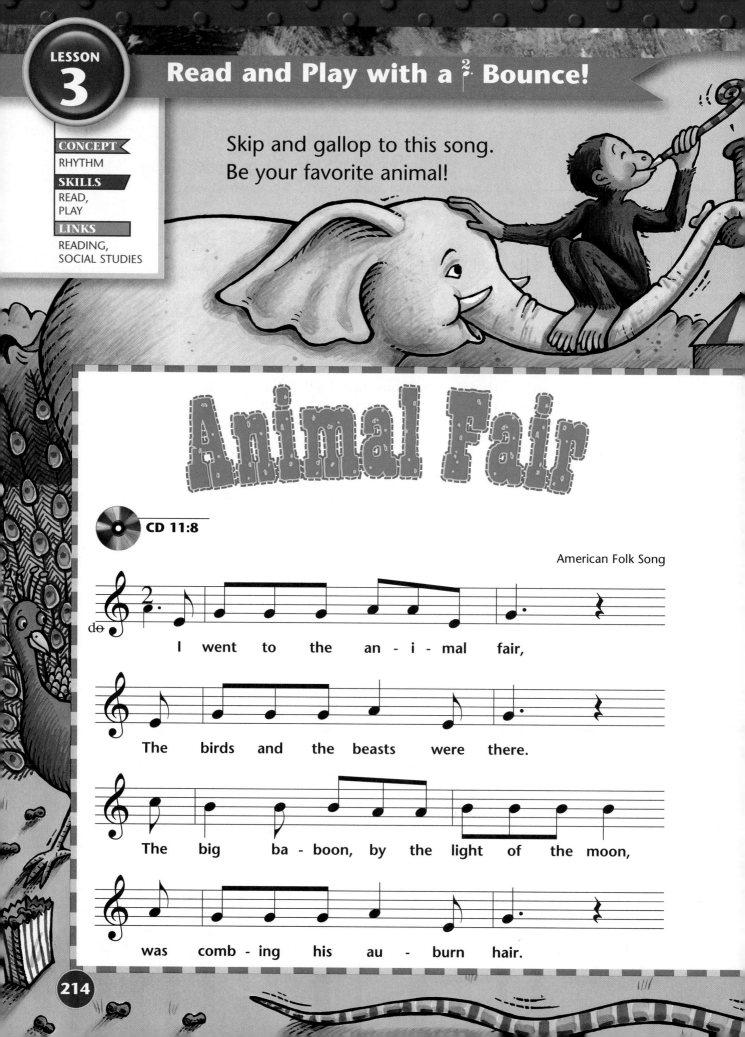

Read and Play with a ²₄ Bounce!

CONCEPT
RHYTHM
SKILLS
READ, PLAY
LINKS
READING, SOCIAL STUDIES

Skip and gallop to this song.
Be your favorite animal!

Animal Fair

CD 11:8

American Folk Song

I went to the an - i - mal fair,

The birds and the beasts were there.

The big ba - boon, by the light of the moon,

was comb - ing his au - burn hair.

Read the pattern below using animal names.
Play the pattern on any rhythm instrument
as you sing the song.

Playalong

You ought to have seen the monk;

He climbed up the el - e - phant's trunk.

The el - e - phant sneezed and fell on her knees,

and what be - came of the monk?

At Sea and at the Barber's in $\frac{2}{4}$

Have you ever gone to sea?

Read the rhythm of this song. Find the words that rhyme.

Play this pattern ♪♪♩ ♩. on *sea*, *me*, and *three* as you sing the song.

Going Over the Sea

CD 11:11

Canadian Street Rhyme

Verse

de

1. When I was one I ate a bun,
2. When I was two I buck-led my shoe,
3. When I was three I banged my knee,   } Go-ing o-ver the sea.
4. When I was four I shut the door,
5. When I was five I learned to jive,

I jumped a-board a sail-or-man's ship, And the sail-or-man said to

Refrain

me, "Go - ing o - ver, go - ing un - der, Stand at at -

ten - tion like a sol - dier, With a one, two, and three."

6. When I was six I picked up sticks, . . .

7. When I was seven I went to heaven, . . .

8. When I was eight I learned to skate, . . .

9. When I was nine I climbed a vine, . . .

10. When I was ten I caught a hen, . . .

What does a barber do? *The Barber of Seville* is an opera about a smart and funny barber. His name is Figaro.

When one person sings a solo in an opera, it is called an **aria**. In this aria Figaro sings about how busy he is. People are always ordering him around.

Fi - ga - ro quà
Fi - ga - ro here

Read this pattern. Raise your hand when you hear this rhythm pattern in the aria.

 LISTENING CD 11:14

Largo al factotum from
Il Barbiere di Siviglia
(The Barber of Seville)
by Gioachino Rossini

Figaro in
The Barber of Seville

LOG ON

See music.mmhschool.com to research opera.

CONCEPT
MELODY
SKILLS
IMPROVISE,
NOTATE, SING
LINKS
SCIENCE,
CULTURES, DANCE

See
music.mmhschool.com
to research Korean
music.

The moon can look different at different times of the month. Some people think the moon looks like a boat.

Read this poem. Speak it again as you **play**. **Improvise** using *do re mi so* and *la*.

Moon Boat

Moon Boat, little, brave and bright,
Tossed upon the seas of night,
One day when I'm free to roam,
I'll climb aboard and steer you home.

Charlotte Pomerantz

Art Gallery

The Sun Rises While the Moon Sleeps
by Peter Davidson

This song describes the way a crescent moon in Korea looks like a boat sailing in the sky.

MAP

UNITED STATES

KOREA

BAN DAL

Half Moon

CD 11:15

Words and Music by Keuk Young Youn
English Words by Linda Worsley

Korean: 푸 른 하 늘 은 – 하 수 하 얀 쪽 배 엔
English: Sky of blue, and glit-ter-ing moon, Lit-tle boat so white;—

계 수 나 무 한 – 나 무 토 끼 한 마 리
On your hull a cin-na-mon tree, sail-ing through the night.—

돛 대 도 아 니 달 고 삿 대 도 없 이
On your bow, a rab-bit runs, lit-tle boat so high,—

가 기 도 잘 도 간 다 서 – 쪽 나 라 로
With-out a sail or rud-der, tra-vel-ing through the sky.___

Step Back with *Do Re Mi So* and *La*

Move down the "alley" as you sing this song.
What pitches are in this song? Write them.

1 **Sing** and **move** with the song. Pick a partner and form an "alley." Swing your arms with the beat on the first verse.

2 Step back and clap with the beat on the second verse. One person moves down the alley.

3 Continue clapping and singing. The other partner moves down the alley on the third verse.

Rondo

CONCEPT
FORM
SKILLS
ANALYZE,
SING, LISTEN
LINKS
SCIENCE

Shoo the flies away as you **listen** to this song. What is the form of the song?

In music a **fermata** tells you to hold the note longer.

Find the ⌒ in the song. **Sing** the song.

SHOO, FLY

CD 11:22

American Folk Song

Ⓐ

Shoo, fly, don't both-er me, Shoo, fly, don't both-er me,

Shoo, fly, don't both-er me, For I be-long to some-bod-y.

Ⓑ

I feel, I feel, I feel, I feel like a morn-ing star,

I feel, I feel, I feel, I feel, I feel like a morn-ing star.

Some music has different sections between each A section. The form of music that does this is called a **rondo**. One kind of rondo form is ABACA.

The form of "Shoo Fly" is ABA. **Create** a rondo by adding a C section to "Shoo, Fly." **Sing** the song and add a hand jive to create the new C section.

Hand Jive

cool wave

hitch hike

champ cheer

THEN...

1. CATCH A FLY
2. PUT IT IN YOUR HAND
3. THROW IT ON THE FLOOR
4. STEP ON IT

catch a fly

A Oh, Shoo, fly, don't both-er me, Shoo, fly, don't both-er me,

Shoo, fly, don't both-er me, For I be-long to some-bod-y.

Piano Music in Rondo Form

You have to practice many hours to become a great musician. Evgeny Kissin is a very talented classical pianist.

Meet the Musician

Evgeny Kissin was born in Moscow, Russia, in 1971. He began to play the piano when he was two years old. He has performed all over the world.

RECORDED INTERVIEW CD 11:25

Listen to Evgeny Kissin talk about playing the piano.

THINK! What do you think helped Evgeny Kissin become a great pianist?

Did you ever get really angry over losing something? In this music someone is angry because he or she lost a penny. This music is in rondo form.

LISTENING CD 11:26

Rondo a capriccio (Rage over a Lost Penny) by Ludwig van Beethoven

Follow the map as you **listen**.

Listening Map for Rondo a Capriccio

| A | B | A | C | A |

Listen again. **Move** to show the different sections of ABACA form.

Meet the Musician

Ludwig van Beethoven is considered one of the greatest composers who ever lived. Beethoven's father was a singer and musician and was Ludwig's first teacher. Beethoven was only 12 when he wrote and published his first music. He began to lose his hearing when he was 30. Even though he could not hear his pieces performed, Beethoven could hear the music in his head. He composed some of his greatest works after he was completely deaf.

Instrument Families

CONCEPT
INSTRUMENTAL
TONE COLOR

SKILLS
ANALYZE,
SING, LISTEN

LINKS
CULTURES

You can find many instruments at the market in San Juan, Puerto Rico.

What instruments do you hear in this song? How is the sound of each instrument different?
Sing the song.

MAP

UNITED STATES

PUERTO RICO

En la feria de San Juan

In the Market of San Juan

CD 11:27

Puerto Rican Folk Song
English Version by MMH

Verse

do

Spanish: En la fe - ria de San Juan, yo com - pré un pi -
English: In the mar - ket of San Juan, I___ bought my-self a

Cumulative

tí - o, pi - ti, pi - ti, pi - ti, el pi - tí - o.
whis - tle, *(whistle the melody)*——— the whis - tle.

Refrain

Ven - ga_u - sted, ven - ga_u - sted, a la fe - ria de San Juan,
Come with me, come with me, to the mar - ket of San Juan.

Refrain

Ven - ga u - sted,   ven - ga u - sted,   a   la   fe - ria   de   San   Juan.
Come with   me,   come with   me,   to   the   mar-ket   of   San   Juan.

2. En la feria de San Juan
   yo compré un tambor.
   Ton, ton, ton, el tambor, . . .

   In the market of San Juan
   I bought myself a drum.
   Tum, tum, tum, tum, the drum . . .

3. yo compré una guitarra,
   tara, tara, tara, la guitarra . . .

   I bought a guitar,
   tara, tara, tara, the guitar . . .

4. yo compré un violín,
   Lin, lin, lin, el violín, . . .

   I bought a violin,
   Lin, lin, lin, the violin, . . .

Meet the Orchestral Instrument Families

The instruments of the orchestra are grouped in families. The families are **woodwinds**, **brass**, **strings**, and **percussion**. **Listen** to instruments from each family. Point to each instrument when you hear it.

CD-ROM

Use *Orchestral Instruments* **CD-ROM** to learn more about orchestral instruments.

Orchestral Instrument Families

Woodwinds

flute

piccolo

clarinet

oboe

English horn

bassoon

Brass

trumpet

French horn

trombone

tuba

Find each instrument family on these pages as you **listen** to this music.

LISTENING — CD 12:1

Young Person's Guide to the Orchestra
by Benjamin Britten

THINK! How are the instruments in each family alike? How are they different?

Strings

violin   viola   cello   double bass   harp

Percussion

timpani   xylophone   bass drum   gong   snare drum

229

LESSON
7

CONCEPT
MELODY
SKILLS
LISTEN, SING,
CREATE
LINKS
CULTURES,
READING,
SCIENCE

Steps, Skips, and Leaps

Melodies can move by steps, skips, and leaps.

One pitch to the next one higher or lower is called a **step**.

Skips are from line to line or space to space.

Any jump larger than a skip can be called a **leap**.

Find a step, skip, and leap in this Native American song. **Sing** the song.

NIKOSI

Bluebirds

CD 12:2

Hopi Children's Song
As Sung by Angela Fields

Hopi: ah   ah   ni - ko - si   ah   ah   ni - ko - si

At the end of 2nd time song is sung in the story, pitches are spoken, in a faster tempo.

ah   ah   ni - ko - si   ah - ah   ni - ko - si   ah   ah   ah   ah   ah

This song is part of the Hopi story "Coyote and the Bluebirds." **Listen** to the story and **sing** the song.

🔘 **LISTENING** CD 12:4

Coyote and the Bluebirds Hopi Children's Story as told by Angela Fields

Follow the story pictures as you listen.

Learn About the Hopi Nation

The Hopi are a group of Native Americans who live in northern Arizona. They have always lived in the dry land of Arizona and farming is an important part of their lives.

The Hopi are well known for making beautiful woven baskets, pottery, paintings, and silver jewelry.

Skips and Leaps in the Rain

Rain forests are very thick, wet forests. It rains almost all the time in rain forests. Rain forests are filled with trees, plants, and animals.

"La lluvia" means "the rain" in Spanish. **Listen** to two main melodic ideas in this music. Which moves in leaps and which moves in steps?

a.

b.

Listen to *La lluvia*. Tell what you hear.

🔘 **LISTENING** CD 12:5

La lluvia by Stephen Hatfield

Listen to the music again. **Move** as a rain-forest animal with steps, skips, or leaps.

Meet the Musician

Stephen Hatfield is a composer from British Columbia, Canada. He was raised near a rain forest. This music is about a rain forest.

Sing this song about rain.

It's Raining! It's Pouring!

CD 12:6

Anonymous

SO

It's rain - ing. It's pour - ing. The old man is snor - ing.

He bumped his head and went to bed and did-n't get up 'til morn-ing.

Create a "Rain Rondo." Use "It's Raining! It's Pouring!" for the A section. Choose one song below for the B section and one song for the C section.

Alto Xylophone

① Rain on the green grass and rain on the tree.

Rain on the house - tops, but not on me!

Bass Xylophone

② Rain be - fore sev - en will

clear by e - lev - en.

Play instruments and sing your "Rain Rondo."

233

The Shape of the Melody

CONCEPT
MELODY
SKILLS
LISTEN,
DESCRIBE, SING
LINKS
CULTURES,
SCIENCE,
READING

Global Voices

This is a song that children in Ghana, Africa, like to sing. "Tue Tue" is the name of a rice dish. **Listen** and **move** to show the shape of this music.

MAP

UNITED STATES   GHANA   UGANDA

LISTENING CD 12:9

Tue Tue collected by Akosua Addo

Tue Tue Maria Tue Tue
Tue Tue Maria Tue Tue
Abosom daa, Ama na wa ye
Tue Tue
Abosom daa, Ama na wa ye
Tue Tue la la la

Learn to speak Akan:

Good morning.	Mema wo akye.
Good-bye.	Nante yie.
My name is …	Me din de …
Thank you.	Meda wo ase.
You are welcome.	Yenni aseda.

This song is from Uganda, Africa. **Move** to show the shape of the melody as you listen.

LISTENING CD 12:10

Mwiji Mwena

Traditional African spiritual sung by the African Children's Choir

Clap with the beat as you **listen** again. Clap four beats to the right, then four beats to the left.

African Children's Choir

235

The Shape of Growing Things

Have you ever planted a flower garden? Are the lines in this painting of flowers curved or straight?

Art Gallery

Irises by Vincent van Gogh

Vincent van Gogh was a painter from the Netherlands. He painted this picture of irises in a flower garden in France.

Sing this song about a garden.
Show the shape of the melody with your hands.

Garden Song

CD 12:11

Words and Music by David Mallett

1. Inch by inch, row by row,____
2. Pull - in' weeds and pick - in' stones,_
3. Plant your rows straight and long,____

Gon - na make this gar - den grow,____
We are made of dreams and bones,
Temp - er them with prayer and song,

All it takes is a rake and a hoe
Feel the need to____ grow my____ own
Moth - er Earth will____ make you____ strong,

and a piece of fer - tile ground.____
'cause the time is close at hand.____
if you give her love and care.____

Inch by inch, row by row,____
Grain for grain, sun and rain,____
Old crow watch-ing hun - gri - ly____

Some - one bless the seeds I sow,
Find my way in na - ture's chain,
From his perch in yon - der tree.

Some - one warm them from be - low____
Tune my bod - y and my brain____
In my gar - den I'm as free____

'til the rain comes tum - bl - ing down.
to the mu - sic from____ the land.
as that feath - ered thief____ up there.

Spotlight Your Success!

REVIEW

1 Which shows the pitches in a pentatonic scale?

a.

b.

2 Which rhythm shows three sounds to a beat in $\frac{2}{\bullet\cdot}$?

a. ♩ ♩ ♩   b. ♪ ♪ ♪   c. ♩ ♩ ♩

READ AND LISTEN

1 **Read** these patterns. Which one do you hear?

a.

b.

2 **Read** these patterns. Which one do you hear?

a.

b.

THINK!

1. Tell what an aria is and how it is different from a folk song.

2. Name the four instrument families. Pick two and tell how they are alike and different.

3. **Choose** a song you liked in this unit. Write about why you liked it.

CREATE AND PERFORM

1. Create a pattern two measures long.

   - Write in $\frac{2}{4}$ meter.

   - Use only *so* and *la*.

2. **Play** your pattern as you sing "All Around the Buttercup."

Spotlight on Music Reading

Quarter Notes and Eighth Notes

Read the rhythm. Play a game about stirring chocolate.

Bate, Bate

CD 12:15

Mexican Game

$\frac{2}{4}$

Spanish: **Ba** - te, ba - te, cho - co - la - te,

Con ar - roz y con to - ma - te.

U - no, dos, tres,   CHO,
                      CO,

U - no, dos, tres,   LA,
                      TE,

Cho - co - la - te, cho - co - la - te,

Cho - co - la - te, cho - co - la - te.

So and *Mi*

Sing these pitches. Follow the hands up and down.

Read the whole song with pitch names.
Sing it with the words.

so   so

mi   mi

so   so

mi

SAY YOUR NAME

CD 12:19

Music by Marilyn Copeland Davidson
Words by Sue Snyder

Say your name and when you do,

We will say it back to you.

Play the game!

UNIT 1 READING

CONCEPT
MELODY
SKILLS
READ, SING

Read and Listen for *So* and *Mi*

Sing *so* and *mi* in this song in a new place.

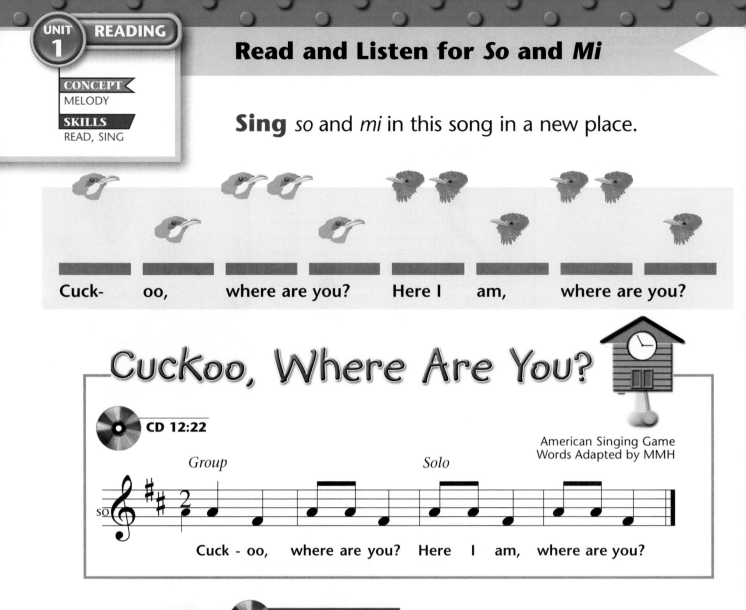

Cuck- oo, where are you? Here I am, where are you?

Cuckoo, Where Are You?

CD 12:22

American Singing Game
Words Adapted by MMH

Group   *Solo*

Cuck - oo,   where are you?   Here   I   am,   where are you?

LISTENING CD 12:25

Im Krapfenwaldl (In Krapfen Woods), Op. 336
by Johann Strauss, Jr.

Listen and point to each section as you hear it.
Move when you hear the cuckoo call, *so-mi.*

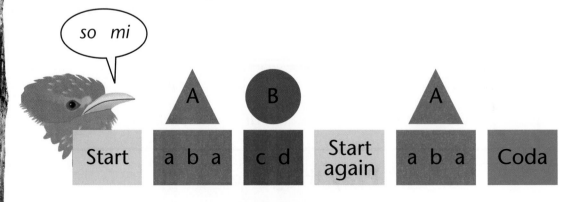

so   mi

Start | A: a b a | B: c d | Start again | A: a b a | Coda

244

UNIT 1 READING

So-Mi Games and the Silent Beat

CONCEPT
MELODY
SKILLS
READ, SING

Read these pitches.
Sing each song and play the games.

Hey, Hey, Look at Me

CD 12:26

American Singing Game
Words Adapted by MMH

Hey, hey, look at me, Make your-self look just like me.

so   mi   so so mi

In and Out

CD 12:29

American Folk Song

In and out, 'Round a - bout.

O - U - T and that spells out!

245

Listen for *So* and *Mi*

Name three of your favorite outdoor games.
Read these melodies from "Children's Dance."

so

Play   a game! Let's play   a game now!

so

Come,   play!   Come and play with me!

so

Like   to   play Hide and Seek!

How are the melodies alike?
How are they different?
Give each melody a game name.
Listen to the three melodies.
Identify each melody as you listen by
pretending to play that game.

LISTENING CD 12:32

"Children's Dance" from *Merry Mount*
by Howard Hanson

Listen for these melodies in "Children's Dance."

Identify games in the painting.

Children's Games by Pieter Brueghel

Pieter Brueghel liked to paint everyday people having fun. Some of the games in this painting are listed here.

Games
Hand Stands
Blind Man's Bluff
Hoop Game
Riding Barrels
Leap Frog
Get the Hat
Tug-of-War
Odds and Evens

Read these game rhythms.

Leap Frog,   Tug - of - War,   Odds and E - vens, Hoop Game.

Choose games from the list.
Create a song using *so* and *mi*.

247

Sing with *La*

Find *la* in this song.

Read the pitches of this song.
Sing the song with the words.

Plainsies, Clapsies

CD 12:33

American Folk Song

Plain - sies,   clap - sies,   twirl a - round to   back - sies,

Right hand,   left hand, stretch it high,   stoop it low,

Touch your knee, touch your toe, touch your heel and 'round you go.

CONCEPT
MELODY

SKILLS
READ, SING

Leap from *Mi* to *La*

Sing the *mi-la* leaps in these songs.

Beats with No Sound

Find the beats with no sound.
Read the rhythm of the song.
Say "yum-my" for ♫
Say "treat" for ♩

Sing the song.

Eating Lizards

CD 12:42

Words and Music by Carol Huffman

Bil - ly Iz - zard ate some liz - ards. Tossed their tails in

gar - bage pails. Bil - ly's broth - er ate an - oth - er.

Got in trou - ble with his moth - er.

No more liz - ards for the Iz - zards!

Find 𝄾 in the song.
Sing the song and solve the riddles.

Riddle Song

CD 12:45

Words and Music by
Marilyn Copeland Davidson

Refrain

Rid - dles   are such fun!   Can   you   tell me one?

Verse

1. I   have   let - ters,   one   two   three,
2. 'Til   I'm   meas - ured,   I'm   not   known,

Add   two   more   and   few - er there will   be.
But   you'll   miss   me   when a - way I've flown.

Step the rhythm of the first line of "Riddle Song."
Bend forward on measures 1 and 3.
Bend back on measures 2 and 4.

Now you know part of a folk dance from Bolivia.

 LISTENING CD 13:1

Carnavalito (Bolivian folk dance) performed
by the Shenanigans

Move your feet as you listen to "Carnavalito."
Stay still on each 𝄾

Sing with *Do*

Do, mi, and *so* all sit on lines or in spaces.

do

do mi so   do mi so

Who Has the Penny?

CD 13:2

American Singing Game

Question: Who has the pen - ny?   Who has the pin?
Answer: I have the pen - ny.   I have the pin.

Heigh Ho, Here We Go

CD 13:5

American Folk Song

Heigh   ho,   here   we   go,

Up   and   down   and   high   and   low.   We're

rid - ing   on   a   see - saw.

Sing a *mi-do* cuckoo call.

mi   do

🔘 **LISTENING** **CD 13:8**

Cuckoo in the Heart of the Woods from
Carnival of the Animals by Camille Saint-Saëns

Listen to "Cuckoo in the Heart of the Woods."

Tap each footprint and cuckoo to follow the path.

Listening Map for Cuckoo in the Heart of the Woods

More Practice with *Do*

Both of these songs have *so*, *mi*, and *do*.

Read *so*, *mi*, and *do* then sing the songs.

Mother, Mother

CD 13:9

Swing (♫ = ♩♩)

American Jump Rope Game

do

1. Moth - er, Moth - er, I am sick.
2. In came the doc - tor, In came the nurse,
3. I don't want the doc - tor, I don't want the nurse,
4. Out went the doc - tor, Out went the nurse,

Call for the doc - tor Quick, quick, quick!
In came the la - dy with the al - li - ga - tor purse.
I don't want the la - dy with the al - li - ga - tor purse.
Out went the la - dy with the al - li - ga - tor purse.

Mouse, Mousie

CD 13:12

Hungarian Folk Song

do

Mouse, Mou - sie, lit - tle mou - sie, hur - ry, hur - ry do!

Or the kit - ty in the hou - sie will be chas - ing you!
(RUN!)

Sing with *La*

Find *la* on the staff, on the stairs, and in the song.
Read the pitches in this song.
Sing the song and play the game.

do mi so la

la
so
mi
do

Daisy Chain

CD 13:15

American Singing Game

Chain, chain, dai - sy chain, All the pret - ty flow - ers,

One for you, and one for me, and one for Jen - ny Bow - ers.

Read and Sing Half Notes

A half note ♩ is a sound that lasts for two beats.
♩♩ = ♩

Find the half notes in this song.
Read all of the rhythms and pitches.
Sing the song with the words.

Donkey, Donkey

CD 13:18

Old English Rhyme
Music by Margaret Campbelle-Holman

Don-key, don-key, old and gray, O-pen your mouth and gent-ly bray.

Lift your eyes, blow your horn, Wake the world this sleep-y morn.

Say this pattern as others sing the song.

Bray, bray, don-key, bray.

Create up your own donkey song using these rhythms and *do mi so la*.

CONCEPT
MELODY
SKILLS
READ, SING

Read the pitches. Sing these songs.

King's Land

CD 13:21

American Folk Song

do

I'm on the king's land, the king is not at home.

He's gone to Bos - ton, to buy his wife a comb.

MR. FROG

CD 13:24

American Singing Game

do

On a log, Mis - ter Frog sang a song the whole day long,

Glumph, Glumph, Glumph.

Sing with *Re*

Re is between *mi* and *do*. **Find** and sing the yellow *mi re do* patterns. **Read** the pitches and sing both songs.

re

Hot Cross Buns

CD 13:27

English Street Cry

Hot cross buns, hot cross buns,

One a pen-ny, two a pen-ny, hot cross buns.

Hop, Old Squirrel

CD 13:30

Virginia Folk Song

Hop, old squirrel, Ei - dle dum, ei - dle dum,

Hop, old squirrel, Ei - dle dum, dee! Ei - dle dum, dee!

Read *Mi Re Do*

This Japanese song is about a bottomless pot.
Read and sing these pitches and rhythms.

Name the starting and ending pitch.
Read and sing the song.

Nabe, Nabe, Soku, Nuke

Stewpot, Stewpot, Bottomless Pot

CD 13:33

Bottomless Pot

Japanese Singing Game
English Version by MMH

Japanese: な　べ　な　べ　そ　こ　ぬ　け
English: Stew - pot, stew - pot, bot - tom - less pot;

そ　こ　が　ぬ　け　た　ら　か　え　り　ま　しょう
Now we turn it up - side down and emp - ty out the pot!

Sing *Do Re Mi So*

"Rover" is a dog's name.

Sing *do re mi so* up and down the stairs.

Find the half note.
Read the song with syllables then sing it.

Rover

CD 13:37

Music by Denise Bacon
Traditional English Rhyme

do

1. I have a dog, and his name is Ro - ver.
2. When he is good, he is good all o - ver.

He is the one I love the best.
When he is bad, he is just a pest.

Think of another name for a pet. Use it to sing the song again.

UNIT 4 READING

CONCEPT
MELODY
SKILLS
READ, SING, PLAY

Sing *Do Re Mi So* Game Songs

Find *do re mi so* in both songs.

Find the half notes in the first song.

Who's That Tapping at the Window?

CD 13:40

American Singing Game

1. Who's that tap - ping at the win - dow?
2. I am tap - ping at the win - dow.

Who's that knock - ing at the door?
I am knock - ing at the door.

Matarile

CD 13:43

Mexican Folk Song

Spanish: 1.¿Qué quiere us - ted? Ma - ta - ri - le, ri - le, ri - le.
English: 1.What do you want? Ma - ta - ri - le, ri - le, ri - le.

Quie - ro sal - tar, Ma - ta - ri - le, ri - le, ron.
I want to jump, Ma - ta - ri - le, ri - le, ron.

2. Quiero marchar, . . .
   I want to march, . . .

3. Quiero correr, . . .
   I want to run, . . .

Dotted Half Notes

𝅗𝅥. is a sound that lasts for 3 beats. ♩♩♩ = 𝅗𝅥.

Find the 𝅗𝅥. in this song. How many are there?

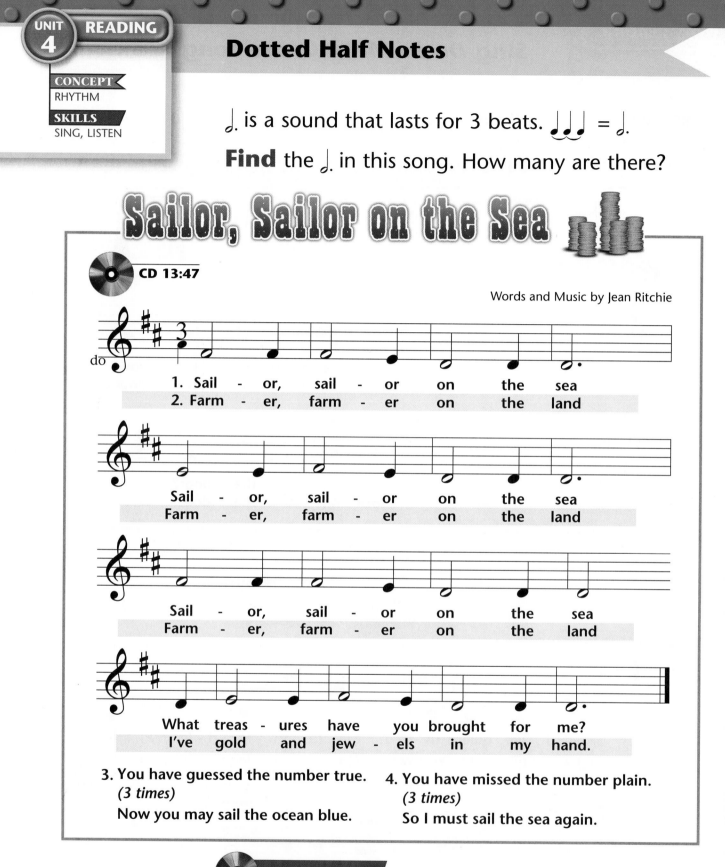

Sailor, Sailor on the Sea

CD 13:47

Words and Music by Jean Ritchie

do

1. Sail - or, sail - or on the sea
2. Farm - er, farm - er on the land

Sail - or, sail - or on the sea
Farm - er, farm - er on the land

Sail - or, sail - or on the sea
Farm - er, farm - er on the land

What treas - ures have you brought for me?
I've gold and jew - els in my hand.

3. You have guessed the number true.
(3 times)
Now you may sail the ocean blue.

4. You have missed the number plain.
(3 times)
So I must sail the sea again.

LISTENING CD 13:50

Sérénade by Cécile Chaminade

Listen to "Sérénade" and sway on each strong beat.

UNIT 5

READING

CONCEPT
MELODY

SKILLS
SING, PLAY

A Pentatonic Song

Penta means five. *Tonic* means tones, or pitches. Pentatonic songs have five tones, or pitches. Sing up and down the pentatonic ladder. Say this pattern with the song.

la

so

mi

re

do

Hey,   hey!   did - dle - um   day!

Here Comes a Bluebird

CD 13:51

American Singing Game

Here   comes a   blue - bird   in   through my   win - dow,

Hey,   did - dle - um - a   day,   day,   day.

Takes him - self   a   part - ner,   hops   in   the   gar - den,

Hey,   did - dle - um - a   day,   day,   day.

Pentatonic Pitches

Sing with pitch syllables then with words.

Dance Together

CD 14:1

American Folk Song

Dance to - geth - er   one by one,   two by two;

Live - ly   mu - sic   calls to me,   calls to you.

Read and play this rhythm with the song.

Bow, Wow, Wow

CD 14:4

Mother Goose Rhyme

"Bow,   wow,   wow!"   "Whose   dog   art   thou?"

"Lit - tle Tom - my   Tuck - er's dog.   Bow,   wow,   wow!"

Read These Songs

Find the pitches and sing the songs.

Pairs or Pears

CD 14:7

English Folk Song

do

Twelve pairs hang-ing high, Twelve knights rid-ing by.

Each knight took a pear, And yet left a doz-en there.

Knock the Cymbals

CD 14:10

Traditional Play-Party Song

do

1. Knock the cym-bals, do, oh do, Knock the cym-bals,
2. Left hand crossed,_ do, oh do, Left hand crossed,_

do, oh do, Knock the cym-bals, do, oh do, Oh-law, Su-sie gal.
do, oh do, Left hand crossed,_ do, oh do, Oh-law, Su-sie gal.

3. Right hand crossed, . . .   4. Promenade around, . . .

Rhythms in ²⁄₄.

A dot after a note makes it longer.

♪♪♪ = ♩.

In ²⁄₄. each of these rhythms gets one beat.

♩.   ≹   ♪♪♪   ♩♪

Sing this song and play the game.

CD 14:13

American Folk Song

1. I see, as plain as can be,

Some-thing that starts with "P." _____ Pen - cil.

2. . . . "D." Desk.
3. . . . "R." Ruler.
4. . . . "T." Table.

LISTENING CD 14:19

Merry-Go-Round by Georges Bizet.

Listen for rhythms in ²⁄₄. "Les chevaux de bois."

266

Read in ²⁄₈.

Read and sing this pentatonic song in ²⁄₈ meter.

Merry-Go-Round

CD 14:16

Music by Marilyn Copeland Davidson
Words by Dorothy Baruch

I climbed up on the mer - ry - go - round And
I climbed up on a big___ brown horse and

it went 'round and 'round.
it went up and down.

'Round and 'round and up and down, I sat high up on a

big brown horse And rode a - round on the mer - ry - go - round And

rode a - round on the mer - ry - go - round. I rode a - round on the

mer - ry - go - round, A - round and 'round and 'round.

accelerando poco a poco

rit. poco a poco

ritard. al Fine

Game Songs in 2. Meter

Read the rhythms of these songs in 2. meter.

CD 14:20

Oliver Twist

American Folk Song

so

O - li-ver Twist, you can't do this, So what's the use of try - ing;

Touch your knees, touch your toes, Clap your hands and a - round you go!

SALLY GO 'ROUND THE SUN

CD 14:23

Nursery Rhyme

do

Sal - ly go 'round the { sun. / moon.

Sal - ly go 'round the chim - ney tops

Ev - 'ry af - ter - noon. Boom!

Listen for ²⁄₈⋅ Patterns

Gigue is the French word for jig. A jig is a quick dance in ²⁄₈⋅ meter.

LISTENING CD 14:26

Gigue

by Johann Sebastian Bach

Listen for these ²⁄₈⋅ patterns and follow the listening map.

♩. ♩♪ ♫♫

Listening Map for Gigue

CONCEPT
RHYTHM
SKILLS
READ, SING, PLAY

Read and Play $\frac{2}{4}$ Rhythms

Sing this song and learn the game.

Juan Pirulero

CD 14:27

Folk Song from New Mexico

Spanish: Es - te es el jue - go de Juan Pi - ru - le - ro;
English: This is the game of *Juan Pi - ru - le - ro;*

Que ca - da quien a - tien - da a su jue - go.
Ev - 'ry - one lis - ten, learn how to play it.

Read and play these patterns with the song.

Playalong

Play!   Learn how to

Learn to play!   Learn to play!

Juan Pi - ru - le - ro!

Play!   Play!   Play!   Play!

CONCEPT
RHYTHM
SKILLS
CREATE

A Bird Sings in ²⁄₄

Read this poem with rhythms.

I Heard a Bird Sing

I heard a bird sing,
In the dark of December
A magical thing
And sweet to remember,
"We are nearer to spring
Than we were in September."
I heard a bird sing in the dark of December.

— *Oliver Herford*

Create a melody for the poem,
using *do re mi so la.*
Who will sing the solo bird part?

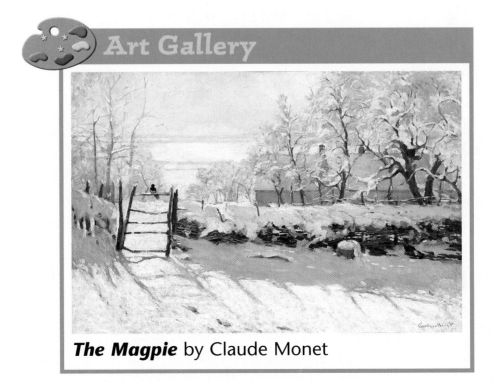

Art Gallery

The Magpie by Claude Monet

271

Spotlight on Performance

Broadway For Kids

MTI's BROADWAY junior

SEUSSICAL

Mini musicals specifically designed for classroom study and presentation, featuring scenes and songs from the musical Seussical Junior.

ADMIT ONE 0596033

Music by Stephen Flaherty
Lyrics by Lynn Ahrens
Book by Lynn Ahrens and Stephen Flaherty
Co-Conceived by Lynn Ahrens, Stephen Flaherty, and Eric Idle
Based on the Works of Dr. Seuss

Musical Numbers

Oh, the Thinks You Can Think!

Horton Hears a Who!

Horton Hears a Who! Two

It's Possible

Green Eggs and Ham

Seussical Mega-Mix

About Rehearsals

You are about to begin rehearsals for a mini production of *Seussical Junior*. **Rehearsing** means learning and practicing something. Below are some words actors use during rehearsals.

Upstage

The area farthest away from the audience.

Stage right

The area to the actor's RIGHT as she or he faces the audience.

Stage left

The area to the actor's LEFT as she or he faces the audience.

Downstage

The area onstage closest to the audience.

About the Script

CHARACTER NAMES are colored **RED**

DIALOGUE is colored **BLUE**

STAGE DIRECTIONS are colored *GREEN*

NARRATOR: It's great to learn something
new and exciting
So we'd like to present
something fun and inviting;
With rhymes running wild and
out on the loose,
Of course they were written
by—who?

KIDS: DR. SEUSS!

Oh, the Thinks You Can Think!

CD 14:31

Music by Stephen Flaherty
Lyrics by Lynn Ahrens

All

Oh, the Thinks you can think!   Oh, the Thinks you can think

if you're will-ing to try.___   Think in-vis-i-ble ink!

Or a Gink with a stink!   Or a stair to the sky!_____

If you o-pen your mind,   oh, the Thinks you will find lin-ing up to get loose...___   Oh, the Thinks you can think

when you think a - bout   Seuss!

NARRATOR: *(To the KIDS)*
We'll take a few stories and
cook up a stew.
Which Dr. Seuss story
would you like to do?

KIDS (Group 1): "If I Ran the Zoo."

KIDS (Group 2): Or "Solla Sollew."

KIDS (Group 3): How about Horton who heard
the small Who?

NARRATOR: "Horton Hears a
Who!" is a
great idea.

CHILDREN: HURRAY!

(NARRATOR reads from a book.)

Helen Hayes Youth Theatre, Nyack, NY

NARRATOR: On the eleventh of May
In the Jungle of Nool
In the heat of the day
In the cool of the pool
He was splashing.

KIDS: Splash!

277

NARRATOR: Enjoying the jungle's great joys
When Horton the Elephant
Heard a small noise.

KID 1: Help! Help!

NARRATOR: So Horton stopped splashing.
He looked toward the sound.
"That's funny," thought Horton,
"There's no one around."
Then he heard it again!
Just a very faint yelp
As if some tiny person
    were calling for help.

KID 2: Help! Help!

NARRATOR: "I'll help you," said Horton,
"But who are you, and where?"
He looked and he looked.
He could see nothing there
But a small speck of dust
Blowing past, through the air.
"I say! How confusing! I've never
    heard tell
Of a small speck of dust
    that is able to yell.
So you know what I
    think? Why I
    think that there must
Be someone on top of that
    small speck of dust.
Some poor little person
    who's shaking with fear
That he'll blow in the pool!
He has no way to steer!"

KID 3: He's alone in the universe!

NARRATOR: And Horton the Elephant said:

Horton Hears a Who!

CD 14:32

Music by Stephen Flaherty
Lyrics by Lynn Ahrens

I'll just have to save him be - cause af - ter all, a
per - son's a per - son, no mat - ter how small. A
per - son's a per - son, no mat - ter how small.____

NARRATOR: So, gently and using the greatest
of care
The elephant stretched his great
trunk in the air
And he lifted the dust speck
and carried it over
And placed it down safe
on a very soft clover.

KIDS: Thank you!

NARRATOR: I won't let you down. No, I won't
let you fall.

279

Horton Hears a Who! Two

CD 14:33

Music by Stephen Flaherty
Lyrics by Lynn Ahrens

All

I'll just have to save him be-cause, af - ter all, a per-son's a per-son, no mat-ter how small. A per-son's a per-son, no mat - ter how small.___ Whooo...!_

NARRATOR: Now open your minds—you've got quite a tool. Let's all take a dive in McElligot's pool.

Mis-sus Um-bro - so who's hang-ing out clothes! It's pos-si - ble.

An - y-thing's pos - si - ble! This

might be a riv - er, now might-n't it be, con -

nec-ting Mc-El - li-got's pool with the sea! Then

may-be some fish might be swim-ming, swim-ming toward me!

Oh, the sea is so full of a

num-ber of fish. If a fel-low is pa - tient, he might get his wish! And

that's why I think that I'm not such a fool when I

sit here and fish in Mc - El - li - got's Pool. It's pos - si - ble.

An - y - thing's pos - si - ble! It's

pos - si - ble. An - y - thing's pos - si - ble!

NARRATOR: What have we learned so far from Dr. Seuss?

KID 6: A person's a person, no matter how small.

KID 7: Anything's possible.

KID 8: I hate green eggs and ham?

NARRATOR: How did you learn that? We haven't had green eggs and ham.

KIDS (Group 1): Let's have them now!

KIDS (Group 2): *(Pinching their noses)* Yuck!

Helen Hayes Youth Theatre,
Nyack, NY

Green Eggs and Ham

CD 14:35

Music by Stephen Flaherty
Lyrics by Lynn Ahrens

Group 2

I do not like green eggs and ham._ I

do not like them Sam-I-Am._ I do not like them

here or there._ I do not like them an-y-where. Not

in a house. Not with a mouse. Not here or there. Not

an-y-where. I do not like green eggs and ham! I

Group 1

do not like them, Sam-I-Am! Could_

NARRATOR: *(To audience)* That was a
wonderful story, I say,
But that's all the time that we
have for today.
All kinds of wonderful lessons
were taught
Filling our thinkers with barrels
of thought.
And just to be sure that his
poetry sticks
Let's all sing a big Dr. Seuss
Mega-Mix.

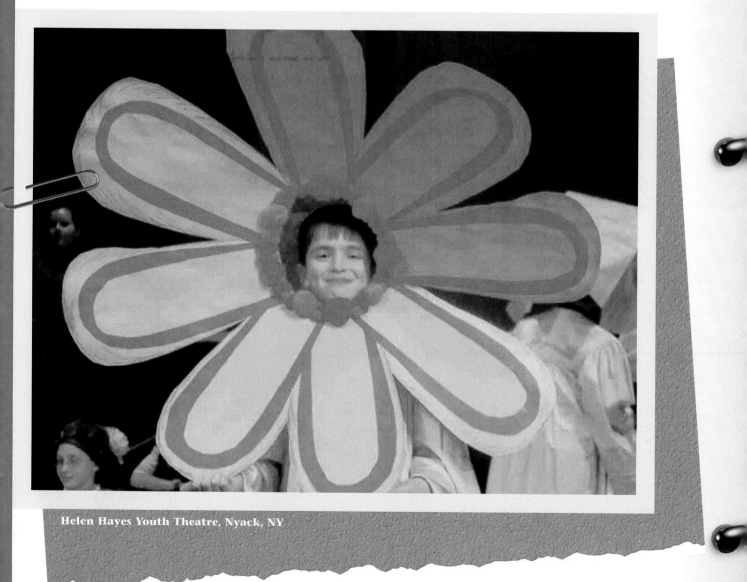

Helen Hayes Youth Theatre, Nyack, NY

Seussical Mega-Mix

CD 14:36

Music by Stephen Flaherty
Lyrics by Lynn Ahrens

Oh, the Thinks you can think! Oh, the Thinks you can think if you're will-ing to try.___ Think in-vis-i-ble ink! Or a Gink with a stink! Or a stair to the sky!___ If you o-pen your mind, oh, the Thinks you will find lin-ing up to get loose...___ Oh, the Thinks you can think when you think a-bout Seuss!

I'll just have to save him be-cause, af-ter all, a per-son's a per-son, no mat-ter how small. A per-son's a

More ➤

per - son,   no   mat - ter   how   small.

Oh,   and that's why   I   think__   that   I'm

not such   a   fool When I   sit here and fish   in Mc -

El - li-got's Pool. It's   pos - si - ble!_____   An - y-thing's

pos - si - ble!_____   I

do not like green eggs and ham._   I   do not like them

Sam-I - Am._   I   do not like them here or there._ I

do not like them an - y-where. Not   in a house. Not

with a mouse. Not here or there. Not an-y-where. I

do not like green eggs and ham! I do not like them,

Sam-I-Am! Seuss! Seuss!

Seuss! I do not like green eggs and ham!

CURTAIN CALL

Meet the Musicians

Lynn Ahrens and **Stephen Flaherty** are the composers of *Seussical*. They have written many different Broadway musicals. Their musicals have won many awards. They also composed the music for the movie *Anastasia*. When Lynn and Stephen decided to compose *Seussical*, they took ideas from many different Dr. Seuss stories. They put them together and created a great new Broadway show!

join us bears in the great out - doors.

Ain't noth-in' like the great out - doors___ to ease your

soul. Ain't noth-in' like the great out - doors___

___ to keep you from grow - in' old.___ If your

mind's been ha - zy and you're feel - in' la - zy 'n'

down on all fours, then join us bears and

suck up some air in the great out - doors.

The Country Bears

CONCEPT
FORM
SKILLS
SING

"Hakuna Matata" is a song from the movie *The Lion King*. In Swahili *hakuna matata* means "no worries." In the movie, Timon and Pumbaa become good friends with Simba. Friends can always help you cheer up.

HAKUNA MATATA

CD 15:1

from the movie
The Lion King

Music by Elton John
Lyrics by Tim Rice

Ha - ku - na ma - ta - ta,

what a won - der - ful phrase!

Ha - ku - na ma - ta - ta, ain't no pass - ing

2nd time to Coda

craze. It means no wor - ries

for the rest__ of your days. It's our

prob-lem - free___ phi - los - o - phy.___

D.C. al Coda

4

Ha - ku - na ma - ta - ta.___

Coda

It means no wor - ries for the rest___ of your

days. It's our prob-lem - free___

phi - los - o - phy.___

2

Ha - ku - na ma - ta - ta.___

Ha - ku - na ma - ta - ta.

CONCEPT
MELODY
SKILLS
SING

In the song "Part of Your World," a young mermaid named Ariel wants to leave the sea and live on land. Did you ever wonder what it would be like to live in a different world? If you lived underwater, you could be friends with sea animals like an octopus and a starfish!

Part of Your World

from the movie *The Little Mermaid*

CD 15:4

Music by Alan Menken
Lyrics by Howard Ashman

I wan-na be___ where the peo-ple are.___
Flip-pin' your fins___ you don't get too far.___

I wan-na see,___ wan-na see 'em danc - in',
Legs are re-quired_____ for jump-in', danc - in'.

walk-in' a-round___ on those, what d' ya call 'em, oh
Stroll-in' a - long___ down the, what's___ that word a - gain,

feet.
street.

Up where they walk, up where they

run, up where they stay all day in the

sun. Wan - der - in' free, wish I could

be part of that world. Up where they

world. Out of the sea, wish I could

be part of that world.

Everyone has someone special that he or she can count on. It might be a friend, a relative, or even a pet. When times are tough, you can be a special person for someone else, too.

Candle on the Water

from the movie *Pete's Dragon*

CD 15:7

Words and Music by Al Kasha
and Joel Hirschhorn

1. I'll be your can-dle on__ the wa - ter,
2. I'll be your can-dle on__ the wa - ter,

my love for you will al-ways burn. I know you're
this flame in-side of me will grow. Keep hold-ing

2nd time to Coda

lost and drift-ing, but the clouds are lift-ing.
on, you'll make it; here's my hand so take it.

Don't give up, you have some-where to turn.

A cold and friend-less tide has found you.

Don't let the storm - y dark - ness pull you down.

I'll paint a ray of hope a - round you,

D.C. al Coda

cir-cling in the air, light-ed by a prayer. ___

Coda

Look for me reach - ing out to show, as sure as riv - ers

flow, I'll nev - er let you go.

I'll nev-er let you go. I'll nev-er let you go.

CONCEPT
MELODY
SKILLS
SING

"It's a Small World" is one of the best-known Disney songs. It reminds you that people may look different on the outside, but they share many of the same feelings.

CD 15:10

Words and Music by Richard M. Sherman
and Robert B. Sherman

Verse

Sing 3 times

It's a world of laugh - ter, a world of

tears; it's a world of hopes and a

world of fears. There's so much that we

share, that it's time we're a - ware, it's a

small world af - ter all.

Zoo-Rific!

Have you ever been to a zoo? Let's take a trip to a musical zoo. We will see birds, bats, horses, elephants, and even little crabs. It will be zoo-rific!

Zoo-Rific!

SKILL BUILDER: Eye Contact and Posture

When you are standing on stage at a concert, there are many interesting things to watch. To be a good performer, keep your eyes on your teacher and stand up straight.

When you sing, try to:

- Stand with your feet shoulder-width apart.
- Keep your back straight.
- Place your hands at your sides.

Let's stop first at the petting zoo. Four pretty white horses are standing in the barn. Here is a great song from the Caribbean we can sing for them!

Four White Horses

CD 15:13

Caribbean Folk Song
Collected by Lois Choksy

Four white hors - es on the riv - er,

Hey, hey, hey, up to - mor - row,

Up to - mor - row is a rain - y day.

Come on up___ to the shal - low bay.

Shal - low bay___ is a ripe ba - nan - a,

Up to - mor - row is a rain - y day.

CONCEPT
MELODY
SKILLS
SING

This zoo has many different kinds of birds. There are parrots, peacocks, ostriches, eagles, and ducks. One little bird is singing her song alone. Sing "Chíu, chíu, chíu" along with her song.

Chíu, chíu, chíu

CD 15:16

Chirp, Chirp, Chirp

Uruguayan Folk Song
English Version by MMH

MAP

UNITED STATES

◀ URUGUAY

Verse

Spanish: **Can-ta, can-ta, pa-ja-ri-to.___ Can-ta, can-ta tu can-**
English: **Can-ta, can-ta, pa-ja-ri-to.___ Sing the songs that cheer me**

ción. **Mi - ra que la vi-da es tris-te y tu can-**
so. **See, my life is full of sor-row, your mer-ry**

tar me a - le - gra el co - ra - zón. **Chí - u, chí - u, chí - u,**
sing-ing sets my heart a - glow. *Chí - u, chí - u, chí - u,*

chí - u,___ chí - u, chí-u, chí-u, chí - u.___ Can - ta, can-ta pa-ja-
chí - u,___ chí - u, chí-u, chí-u, chí - u.___ Can - ta, can-ta pa-ja-

302

ri - to   que tu can - tar me_a - le - gra_el co - ra - zón.
ri - to.   Your mer - ry   sing - ing sets my heart a - glow.

Refrain

Con tus gor - je - os,__ con tu tri - nar,   des - pier - ta_el
Your mer - ry   chirp - ing;__ your roun - de - lay,   You bring the

al - ba,   la no - che   ya se va.   Con tus gor -
dawn - ing,   the shad - ows fade a - way,   Your mer - ry

je - os,_____   con tu tri - nar,_____ des - pier - ta_el
chirp - ing;_____   your roun - de - lay._____ You bring the

al - ba,   la no - che   ya se va.
dawn - ing,   the shad - ows fade a - way.

303

CONCEPT
MELODY
SKILLS
SING

One building at the zoo is very dark inside. There is something furry hanging upside down from the ceiling. What is it?

Leatherwing Bat

CD 15:20

Appalachian Folk Song

1. "Hi!" said the lit - tle leath - er - wing bat,
(Refrain) How - did - dle - dow - dee did - dle - um - day,

"I'll tell you the rea - son that,
How - dee - dow - dee did - dle - um day.

The rea - son that I fly___ by night
Dee - how - dee - dow - dee - did - dle - um - day.

Is be - cause I lost___ my heart's de - light."___
And - a - hey - dee - lee - lee - lye - dee - low.___

2. "Hi!" said the redbird, sitting on a chair,
   "Once I loved a lady fair,
   But she got sassy and from me fled
   And ever since my head's been red."

   Refrain

304

A big favorite at the zoo is the elephant. This song is about an elephant from the country of India.

YANAI

The Elephant

CD 15:23

Words and Music by T. Santhalakshmi
Arranged by M.C. Riley

Tamil: யா னை யா னை யா னை
English: **Ya - nai, Ya - nai, Ya - nai,**

யா ணை பெ ரி ய யா னை
In - di - an e - le - phant Ya - nai.

யா ணை மு கத் தில் தும் பிக் கை
Ro - yal look - ing as a ra - ja,

அ து வே அ தற் கு கை கை கை
Grand and glo - ri - ous as the Taj.

Coda

யா னை யா னை யை னை
Ya - nai, Ya - nai, Ya - nai.

CONCEPT
MELODY
SKILLS
SING

Can you name an animal that can live underwater and walk on land? It is the crab! Here is a song from Brazil about the crab.

MAP

UNITED STATES

BRAZIL

CD 15:27

The Crab

Brazilian Folk Song
English Words by María Luisa Muñoz

Portuguese: **1.** Ca - ran - gue - jo não é pei - xe,
English: **1.** When a crab is in the o - cean,

ca - ran - gue - jo pei - xe é_____
With an un - du - la - ting mo - tion,

Ca - ran - gue - jo não é pei - xe na - da.
He is ve - ry much at home with all the

San - tu da ma - ré.
crea - tures of the sea.

306

¡Pal - ma! pal - ma! pal - ma!
Swish, swish, swish, he swish - es,

¡Pé_____ Pé_____ Pé, Pé!
Down a - mong the fish - es.

Ca - ran - gue - jo só é pei - xe na en -
Oh, a crab is not a fish and yet a

chen - te da ma - ré.
fish he seems to be.

2. Should he take a crabby notion To go walking by the ocean,
   He appears to be no fish at all while crawling on the sand.
   Click, click, click, he's clicking, With his sidewise kicking.
   Oh, a crab is not a fish because no fish can swim on land.

 LISTENING CD 15:31

Batuque na cozinha by Martinho da Vila

Listen to samba music by Martinho da Vila. He is from Brazil, which is where samba music comes from. The rhythm of the drums in samba music makes people want to dance!

CONCEPT
FORM
SKILLS
SING

What would happen if all the animals at the zoo could sing? They would make a super silly group! But no matter how well they could sing, they would all have a place in the choir.

A Place in the Choir

CD 15:32

Refrain

Words and Music by Bill Staines

All God's crit-ters got a place in the choir,

Some sing low, Some sing high - er,

some sing out loud on the tel - e - phone wire,

And some just clap their hands

Fine

or paws or an - y - thing they got now.

Verse

1. Lis - ten to the bass, it's the one on the bot-tom
2. Lis - ten to the top where the lit - tle birds___ sing___
3. It's a sim - ple song of liv - ing sung ev - 'ry - where_

where the bull - frog croaks, and the hip - po - pot - a - mus
On the mel - o - dies with the high notes ring-ing. The
By the ox and the fox and the griz - zly bear,__ The

moans and groans with a big to - do,
hoot owl holl-ers o - ver ev - 'ry - thing
grum-py al - li - ga - tor and the hawk a - bove,

3rd time - D.C. al Fine

And the old cow just goes moo. The
And the jay - bird dis - a - grees.
The sly ra - coon and the dove.

dogs and the cats, they take up the mid -dle,
Sing-in' in the night time, sing - in' in the day__

while the hon - ey - bee hums and the crick - et fid -dles,
The__ lit - tle duck quacks, then he's on his way.__

The don - key brays and the po - ny neighs,
The 'pos - sum ain't got__ much to say

To Refrain

and the old coy - o - te howls.
And the por - cu - pine talks to him - self.

309

Food, Glorious Food!

What is your favorite food? Have you ever been so happy to eat it that you felt like singing? Here are five fun food songs that you can sing anytime, whether you are hungry or not.

VOICE BUILDER: Take a Breath

Good singers make sure they control their breathing. You can learn to control your breathing. Follow these steps:

• Imagine you are holding a giant balloon.
• Pretend to suck all the air slowly out of it.
• Now fill the balloon back up.

GROCERY STORE

OPEN

LISTENING CD 16:4

Food, Glorious Food by Lionel Bart

Listen to this song. What do these children get to eat?

When you are hungry, the best place to go is the grocery store. You can find many kinds of food there. Next time you visit the grocery store, you can sing this song.

Corner Grocery Store

CD 16:1

American Folk Song

There were beans, beans, e-nough to feed ma-rines in the store, in the store. There were beans, beans, e-nough to feed ma-rines in the cor-ner gro-cery store. My eyes are__ dim, I can-not see. I have not__brought my specs with me. I have not__ brought my__ specs with me!

CONCEPT
MELODY
SKILLS
SING

Hooray, look what's for dinner! It is spaghetti, topped with big meatballs and cheese.
Oh no! A meatball rolled off the table.

On Top of Spaghetti

CD 16:5

American Folk Song
Words by Tom Glazer

1. On top of spa - ghet - ti_____
(2.) gar - den_____
(3.) cov - ered_____

All cov - ered with cheese,_____
And un - der a bush,_____
With beau - ti - ful moss;_____

I lost my poor meat - ball_____
And then my poor meat - ball_____
It grew love - ly meat - balls_____

When some - bod - y sneezed.
Was noth - ing but mush.
And to - ma - to sauce.

312

CONCEPT
RHYTHM
SKILLS
SING

The artichoke is a strange vegetable. It does not look friendly, with all those spikes on its leaves! But when it is cooked and dipped in butter, it tastes good enough to sing about!

ARTICHOKES

CD 16:8

Words and Music by Malvina Reynolds

Refrain

Ar - ti-chokes   Mmm mmm   Ar - ti-chokes

(2nd time to Verse 2)
Fine

Mmm mmm   Ar - ti-chokes   Mmm mmm

Verse

1. Down in Mon - ter-rey the ar - ti-chokes grow,

Tow - sy head - ed ar - ti-chokes row af-ter row,

they grow in Mon-ter-rey 'cause it's com - for-ta - ble there,

they like the san - dy bot - tom and the cool salt air.

Verse

2. When you eat an ar-ti-choke you take a lit-tle bite,

Stick you in the fin-ger if you don't hold it right.

Take a lit-tle nib-ble, throw a-way the rest.

D.C. al Fine

E-nough left o-ver for a goo-gle-bir-die's nest.

Piggy

For breakfast I had ice cream
With pickles sliced up in it;
For lunch, some greasy pork chops
Gobbled in a minute;
Dinner? Clams and orange pop,
And liverwurst, slicked thick—
And now, oops! Oh pardon me!
I'm going to be sick!
—*William Cole*

CONCEPT
RHYTHM
SKILLS
SING

People in different parts of the world enjoy different foods. In Croatia, children and adults enjoy eating watermelons.

MAP

UNITED STATES   CROATIA

Ja posejah lubenice

CD 16:11

I Planted Watermelons

Croatian Folk Song
English Version by MMH

Verse

Croatian: 1. Ja po - se - jah lu - be - ni - ce,
English: 1. I am plant - ing wa - ter - mel - ons,

Po - kraj vo - de stu - de - ni - ce,
By the riv - er cool and flow - ing,

Refrain

Se - no, sla - ma, se - no, sla - ma.
Hay and straw, hay and straw,

Zob, zob, zob, zob, zob, zob.
Oats, oats, oats, oats, oats, oats.

2. Seven fields of wheat and barley,
   Nine more fields of corn are planted. *Refrain*

CONCEPT
MELODY
SKILLS
SING

Oranges taste great, and are good for you, too! In Sri Lanka, oranges are a tasty treat. People from Sri Lanka are proud of the oranges they grow.

Me gase boho

MAP
UNITED STATES
SRI LANKA

Orange Tree

CD 16:15

Sinhala Folk Song
English Version by Mary Lu Walker

Sinhala: මේ ග - සේ බො - හෝ පැ - ඩි දො -
English: Or - ange tree bends low. Branch - es are

ඩම් ති - බේ පා - හි - ල ඉ - දි - ලා
touch-ing the ground. Plen - ty of or - ang - es,

ව - ම - ට නෑ - ම් - ලා බ - ර - වෙ - ලා අ - තශෛ
Sweet, juic - y or - ang - es, or - ang - es all a - round.

317

CONCEPT
FORM
SKILLS
SING

Do you know all of the foods in this song? Which food in it is your favorite? Singing about all of these foods can make you hungry. It must be time to eat!

The Food Song

CD 16:19

Words and Music by Jackie Silberg

1. Cap - el - li - ni, fet - tu - ci - ni, es - car - got and bok choy.
2. Wie - ner schnitz - el, salt - ed pret - zels, sau - er - kraut and bok choy.

Jam - ba - lay - a and pa - pay - a, ter - i - yak - i, bok choy.
Moo goo gai pan, en - chi - la - da, sau - er - brat - en, bok choy.

Her - ring, kip - pers, gua - ca - mo - le, krep - lach, crum - pets, rav - i - o - li,

gy - ros, gum - bo, su - shi, cur - ry, poi, bok choy.

Ta - cos,_____ bak - la - va, egg rolls,

french fries,_____ ru - ma - ki, Sal - ly Lunn.

Brat - wurst,_____ la - sa - gna, won ton,

chow mein,__ ce - vi - che, crab ran - goon.   crab ran - goon.

Trip to the Tropics

Pretend you are in the warm tropics in a rain forest. What sounds do you hear? You might hear the sounds of birds, rain, or insects in the forest. Would you like to visit? Pack your bags, because we are taking a musical trip to the tropics!

VOICE BUILDER: Listening

Did you know listening is very important when you sing? Here are some things you need to listen for when you sing. Can you think of any others?

- Instructions from your teacher
- Your own voice
- Other people's voices around you

Jamaica is an island country in the Caribbean Sea. A tree called the banyan tree grows in Jamaica. Banyan trees have roots that grow down from their branches.

Banyan Tree

CD 16:22

Moderately

Jamaican Folk Song

1. Moon shine to - night; come make we dance an' sing.
2. La - dies make curt - sy; gen - tle - men make bow.
3. Then we join hands an' dance a - roun' an' roun'.

Moon shine to - night; come make we dance an' sing.
La - dies make curt - sy; gen - tle - men make bow.
Then we join hands an' dance a - roun' an' roun'.

Me da rock so, you da rock so, un-der ban - yan tree.

Me da rock so, you da rock so, un-der ban-yan tree.

CONCEPT
METER
SKILLS
SING

Fiji is an island country in the Pacific Ocean. In Fiji the water is sky blue and there are many beautiful white-sand beaches. Herons live along streams in Fiji. They are birds with long legs.

MAP

Na belo

CD 16:25

Little Heron

Fijian Folk Song
English Words by Linda Worsley

Fijian: Na be - lo na be - lo___ lai___ lai.
English: Lit - tle her - on came fly - ing to me.

Vu - ka vo - li mai, Va - ka - mu - ri wai. Lai ro
Lit - tle her - on flew down a - long the stream. Then it

i - na ta - ba - ni ti - ri wai. Lai ro!
land - ed a - way up in a tree, Her - on!

(Click, click, click) Lai ro! (Click, click, click)
(Click, click, click) Her - on! (Click, click, click)

CONCEPT
MELODY
SKILLS
SING

People came from all over the world to live in the tropics of Latin America. This is a song some of them sang to celebrate the good things in their lives.

San Sereni

MAP

UNITED STATES

LATIN AMERICA

CD 16:29

Latin American Folk Song

Spanish: 1. San Se - re - ní de la bue - na, bue - na vi - da,

ha - cen a - sí, a - sí los za - pa - te - ros,* a -

sí, a - sí, a - sí, a - sí me gus-ta a mí!

* Sing new word each time through:

1. los zapateros   (the cobblers)
2. las bailadoras   (the folk dancers)
3. los carpinteros   (the carpenters)
4. las pianistas   (the pianists)
5. los campañeros   (the bell ringers)
6. las costureras   (the seamstresses)

CONCEPT
MELODY
SKILLS
SING

Wouldn't it be neat if all birds could talk? If you visit the Tiki Room, you will meet some feathered friends who love to sing and play.

The Tiki Tiki Tiki Room

CD 16:33

Words and Music by Richard M. Sherman
and Robert B. Sherman

In the Ti - ki Ti - ki Ti - ki Ti - ki

Ti - ki Room,_ in the Ti - ki Ti - ki Ti - ki Ti - ki

Ti - ki Room,__ all the birds sing words and the

flow-ers croon_ in the Ti - ki Ti - ki Ti - ki Ti - ki

2nd time to Coda ⊕   Fine

Ti - ki Room._

Wel-come to our trop - i - cal   hide   a - way, ___   you

luck - y   peo - ple   you! ___   If   we

were-n't in the show start-ing right a - way, ___ we'd   be

in   the   aud - i - ence,   too.   All   to-geth-er!

Coda

The   bird of par - a - dise   is   an   el - e-gant bird. ___   It

likes   to   be   seen   and   it   loves   to   be   heard.

Most   lit - tle   bird - ies   will   fly   a - way, ___   but   the

D.C. al Fine

Ti - ki   Room   birds   are   here   ev - 'ry   day.

CONCEPT
TEMPO
SKILLS
SING

For the last stop on our musical trip, we need to take a train. We are going to a city called Caracas in the country of Venezuela. We will travel through the mountains, singing the whole way!

MAP

UNITED STATES

VENEZUELA

CD 16:36

The Train

Venezuelan Folk Song

Spanish: "Pá Ca - ra - cas" di - ce el tren cuan - do
English: "To Ca - ra - cas," says the train when it's

vie - ne de Los Te - ques. "Pá Ca - ra - cas" di - ce el
com - ing from Los Te - ques. "To Ca - ra - cas," says the

tren cuan - do vie - ne de Los Te - ques. Pá Ca -
train when it's com - ing from Los Te - ques. To Ca -

ra - cas, pá Ca - ra - cas, siem - pre lle - ni - to de
ra - cas, to Ca - ra - cas, al - ways ver - y full of

gen - te pa - sa͜a ve - ces por un
peo - ple, some - times pass - ing through a

tu - nel y͜o - tras ve - ces por un puen - te.
tun - nel, some - times pass - ing o - ver bridg - es.

2. When it's going through a tunnel,
it goes very, very slowly.
(Repeat)

Very gently, very slowly,
so the people won't be frightened.
(Repeat)

3. When it crosses over bridges,
it begins to go much faster.
(Repeat)

Hurry, hurry, hurry, hurry,
we're arriving in Caracas!
(Repeat)

LISTENING CD 17:1

Railroad Blues by Freeman Stowers

Sometimes people make their instruments
sound like something else. "Railroad Blues," by
Freeman Stowers, was recorded a long time
ago. He makes his harmonica sound like a train.

Play the music patterns after you read two lines of the poem.

City Traffic

by Betsy Franco

Beep, honk, step on the brake.
City traffic makes us wait.

(any two pitches)

Voice

Out of my way!

Taxis dodging here and there.
Cars and vans are everywhere.

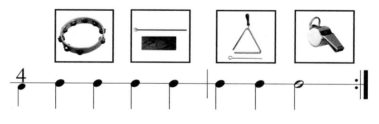

Buses pick up girls and boys.
Trucks look like they're giant toys.

Spoken: **Rol - ling,   rol - ling.**

Blinking stoplights flash and glow.
City traffic's stop and go.

Stop!
(low voice)

Go!
(high voice)

Pull to the right for the siren sound.
Fire trucks are all around.

Traffic stops while a car gets towed.
Lots of people cross the road.

City traffic's really cool,
but I hope that I'm not late for school!

Spoken: **Hold   the bus!**

CONCEPT
RHYTHM
SKILLS
PLAY

Folktale from Mexico

Play the musical part when you see a symbol in the story.

One day Señor Rattlesnake was resting on the nice, warm sand enjoying the sun.

He was almost asleep when a great rock rolled down the hill and landed on top of him.

He wiggled and he jiggled but he could not get out from under it.

"Help! Help!" he whispered. It was so tight he could hardly breathe. A rabbit hopped by and saw the poor snake.

The rabbit had a kind heart, so he pushed the rock and freed the snake.

But when Señor Rattlesnake was free, he opened his mouth to swallow the rabbit for his supper.

"Wait! I just saved you!" cried the rabbit.

"Rabbits-s-s are my favorite treat. You should know better!" laughed Señor Rattlesnake.

While they were talking, Señor Coyote walked over the hill.

Voice

Ah - ooo!

"What is going on here?" asked Señor Coyote. The rabbit and the snake started talking at once.

"Wait, wait," said Señor Coyote. "Take turns talking. Let me judge who is right."

"Señor Rattlesnake was trapped under a rock," explained the rabbit. "I pushed off the rock to help him. Now he wants to eat me!"

"How funny," laughed Señor Rattlesnake. "I was-s-s hiding under the rock to trick the rabbit into helping me. I caught him fair and s-s-square."

"Let's see," said Señor Coyote. "Señor Rattlesnake, show me how you were hiding."

"You must push the rock on top of me s-s-so I can show you," hissed the snake. The rabbit and Señor Coyote pushed the heavy rock back on top of the snake.

"Now do you s-s-see? Help me out now," whispered the snake.

"No, Señor Rattlesnake," said Señor Coyote. "You must learn a lesson about being cruel to those who help you." And they left the rattlesnake there to think about it!

CONCEPT
RHYTHM
SKILLS
PLAY

The Drumming Spider

This story is told in many countries in West Africa. **Play** the music when you see the symbol in the story.

Once upon a time, there was a village where animals and people lived together. The animals could talk, sing, and even play music.

The village had many parties. Spider came to every party. With his eight legs, he could play the most wonderful music on his drums.

But the people in the village did not like to invite Spider and his family. They ate all the food and left nothing for the rest of the guests.

So, when the village chief planned a party for his son's wedding, he did not invite Spider and his family. But Spider's wife found out. She ran home to tell him.

"What? Am I not the best musician at every party?" said Spider. "I'll show them."

On the night of the big party, Spider and his family hid by the stream. Spider brought his drums. And Spider had a plan.

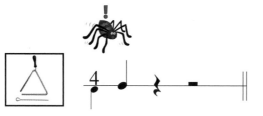

Back at the party, the chief asked a girl to fetch some water at the stream.

Washington Post
by John Philip Sousa

Listen to this piece written for a band.

Some patriotic songs are about our history. "Yankee Doodle" helps us remember our first president, George Washington.

Yankee Doodle

Traditional Melody
Words by Dr. Richard Shuckburgh

CD 17:6

Verse

1. Fath'r and I went down to camp a
2. Yan - kee Doo - dle went to town, a

long with Cap - tain Good - in', and there we saw the
rid - ing on a po - ny, He stuck a feath - er

men and boys as thick as hast - y pud - din'.
in his cap and called it mac - a - ro - ni.

Refrain

Yan - kee Doo-dle keep it up, Yan - kee Doo-dle dan - dy,

Mind the mu - sic and the step, and with the girls be han - dy.

3. There was Captain Washington upon a slapping stallion,
   a-giving orders to his men; I guess there were a million. *Refrain.*

Pat with the steady beat.

There Are Many Flags in Many Lands

CD 17:9

Composer Unknown
Words by M.H. Howliston

There are man-y flags in man-y lands, there are flags of ev-'ry hue; But there is no flag, how-ev-er grand, Like our own Red, White and Blue.

Refrain

Then hur-rah for the flag, Our coun-try's flag, It's stripes and white stars, too; For there is no flag in an-y land, Like our own Red, White and Blue.

Harvest

In autumn, leaves fall everywhere! This is also the season when the crops are gathered.

CD 17:12

Georgia Folk Song

do

1. Time to gath - er har - vest.__ Oh, Em-ma, oh!____

You turn a-round, dig a hole in the ground,_ Oh, Em - ma, oh!

2. Digging sweet potatoes . . .
3. Digging rutabagas . . .
4. Digging big fat parsnips . . .

The apple harvest is in autumn.

How many kinds of apples do you see in your grocery store?

Apple Picker's Reel

CD 17:15

Words and Music by Larry Hanks

do

Hey! Ho! Don't you feel so fine, Look-ing

out a-cross the or-chard in the bright sun-shine.

Hey! Ho! Don't you feel so free,

Stand-ing on the top of the ap-ple tree.

Christopher Columbus sailed across the ocean over 500 years ago.

Find the names of Columbus's three ships in this song.

Columbus Sailed with Three Ships

CD 17:18

Words and Music by Margaret Campbelle-Holman

Co - lum - bus sailed with three ships, three ships,

three ships, Co - lum - bus sailed with three ships

o - ver the o - cean blue._____

Solo   *Group*

The   Ni - ña,   (the   Ni - ña),

Solo   *Group*

the   Pin - ta,   (the   Pin - ta),

Solo

the   San - ta   Ma - rí - a

Group

(the   San - ta   Ma - rí - a),

sailed   the   o - cean   blue._____

CONCEPT
TONE COLOR
SKILLS
SING, CREATE

Halloween is a time when it is fun to pretend.

CD 17:21

Eerily

Words and Music by Teresa Jennings

1. Crea-tures! Mon-sters! Wit-ches! } Hal-low-een!
2. Spook-y! Eer - ie! Creep-y!

{ Spi - ders! Gob - lins! } This is Hal - low - een!
{ Scar - y! Hair - y! }

1.
(Ghosts moaning)

2.
Shout:
(Wolves howling)
Boo!

Create new spooky words.

LISTENING CD 17:24

In the Hall of the Mountain King
from *Peer Gynt Suite* by Edvard Grieg

Describe when the music gets louder.

Some pumpkins are used for decorating. Other pumpkins are used to make pumpkin pie!

Pick a Pumpkin

CD 17:25

Words and Music by Naomi Caldwell

AUTUMN: Thanksgiving

CONCEPT
FORM
SKILLS
LISTEN, SING

Thanksgiving is here! We gather around the table and share food. We give thanks for family and friends.

Listen to an old American song.

 LISTENING CD 17:28

Turkey in the Straw (American folk song)

This fiddle tune became a favorite dance.

At Thanksgiving we are thankful for many things.
Name some things you are thankful for.

Find the rhyming words in this song.

CD 17:29

Music by Franz Schubert

Thank You for the world so sweet,

Thank You for the food we eat,

Thank You for the birds that sing,

Thank You, God, for ev - 'ry - thing.

Seasonal Songs

Snow and ice bring winter fun!

Slide your hands to the steady beat in this song.

Skating

CD 17:32

Words and Music by Lynn Freeman Olson

Glid - ing, glid - ing, Skat-ing a-round the ice.

See how my feet are fly - ing, Noth-ing could be so nice!

Watch me turn - ing smooth and free.

When I am skat-ing I am hap-py as I can be!

Winter Landscape with a Bird Trap

by Pieter Brueghel

This painting was created more than 450 years ago. It shows a winter scene in a village.

Describe what people are doing in this scene.

CONCEPT
TONALITY
SKILLS
LISTEN

Hanukkah is a holiday of lights. It lasts for eight days. A *menorah* holds nine candles. There is one candle for each of the eight nights, and one candle to light the others.

In the Window

CD 17:35

Hebrew Folk Song
English Words by Judith Eisenstein

In the win - dow where you can see the glow

Of my me - no - rah on new - ly fall - en snow,

1. I will set you, one lit - tle can - dle,
2. I will set you, two* lit - tle can - dles,

On this the first night of Ha - nuk - kah.
On this the sec-ond* night of Ha - nuk - kah.

*For each of the nights of Hanukkah, sing the correct number. On the eighth verse, sing the word "last."

At Hanukkah children play with a special top called a *dreidel*.

My Dreidel

CD 18:1

Music by S.E. Goldfarb
Words by S.S. Grossman

1. I have a lit-tle drei-del, I made it out of clay;
2. My drei-del's al-ways play-ful, It loves to dance and spin.

And when it's dry and read-y, Then drei-del I shall play.
A hap-py game of drei-del, Come play, now let's be-gin.

O drei-del, drei-del, drei-del, I made it out of clay;
O drei-del, drei-del, drei-del, It loves to dance and spin.

O drei-del, drei-del, drei-del, Now drei-del I shall play.
O drei-del, drei-del, drei-del, Come play, now let's be-gin.

Holidays often have special music.

 LISTENING CD 18:8

**Chinese Dance from *The Nutcracker Suite*
by Piotr Ilyich Tchaikovsky**

The ballet *The Nutcracker* is a Christmas story.
Clara dreams of adventures with her Nutcracker
doll, a Mouse King, a Snow Queen, and others.

Listen to the music of this famous ballet.

Listening Map for Chinese Dance
from *The Nutcracker*

Introduction
8 beats

8 beats   8 beats

8 beats   8 beats

8 beats   8 beats

Coda

8 beats   8 beats   8 beats

CONCEPT
FORM
SKILLS
SING, PLAY

Pat with the beat as you sing this song.

Find the rhyming words.

Up on the Housetop

CD 18:9

Words and Music by Benjamin T. Hanby

A Verse

do

1. Up on the house - top the rein - deer pause,
2. First comes the stock - ing of lit - tle Nell,
3. Look in the stock - ing of lit - tle Bill,

Out jumps good old San - ta Claus;
Oh, dear San - ta, fill it well.
Oh, just see what a glor - ious fill!

Down through the chim - mey with lots of toys,
Give her a dol - ly that laughs and cries,
Here is a ham - mer and lots of tacks,

All for the lit - tle ones' Christ - mas joys.
One that can o - pen and shut its eyes.
Whis-tle and a ball___ and a whip that cracks.

B Refrain

Ho,   ho,   ho,   Who   would - n't   go?

Ho,   ho,   ho,   Who   would - n't   go? _____

Up   on   the   house - top,   click,   click,   click,

Down through the chim - ney   with   good   Saint   Nick.

Play the rhythm patterns for each section.

A

Tambourine

B

Jingle bells

At Christmas time people like to sing for their neighbors. This is an old carol from England.

We Wish You a Merry Christmas

CD 18:12

MAP

UNITED STATES — ENGLAND

English Carol

1. We wish you a mer - ry Christ - mas,
2. Now bring us some fig - gy pud - ding,
3. For we love our fig - gy pud - ding,

We wish you a mer - ry Christ - mas,
Now bring us some fig - gy pud - ding,
For we love our fig - gy pud - ding,

We wish you a mer - ry Christ - mas,
Now bring us some fig - gy pud - ding,
For we love our fig - gy pud - ding,

And a hap - py New Year.
And____ bring it out here.
So____ bring some out here.

4. We won't go until we get some,
   We won't go until we get some,
   We won't go until we get some,
   So bring some out here.

5. We wish you a merry Christmas,
   We wish you a merry Christmas,
   We wish you a merry Christmas,
   And a happy New Year.

This carol tells the story of a special boat trip.

I Saw Three Ships

CD 18:15

English Carol

1. I saw three ships come sail - ing in,
2. And what was in those ships all three,
3. 'Twas Jo - seph and his fair la - dy,
4. Then all the bells on earth shall ring,

On Christ-mas Day, on

Christ - mas Day;

I saw three ships come sail - ing in,
And what was in those ships all three,
'Twas Jo - seph and his fair la - dy,
Then all the bells on earth shall ring,

On

Christ - mas Day in the morn - ing.

CONCEPT
FORM
SKILLS
SING

This song tells the story of Christmas.

Mary Had a Baby

CD 18:18

Swing (♫ = ♫)

African American Spiritual

1. Ma - ry had a ba - by,
2. What did Ma - ry name him?
3. Ma - ry named him Je - sus,
4. Where was Je - sus born?____

Yes,   Lord,

Ma - ry had a ba - by,
What did Ma - ry name him?
Ma - ry named him Je - sus,
Where was Je - sus born?____

Yes,   my Lord,

Ma - ry had a ba - by,
What did Ma - ry name him?
Ma - ry named him Je - sus,
Where was Je - sus born?____

Yes,   Lord,

The peo - ple keep a - com - ing and the train has gone.

5. Born in lowly stable . . .
6. Where did Mary lay him? . . .
7. Laid him in a manger . . .

360

On Christmas Eve in Mexico, people eat something sweet called *buñuelos*. Buñuelos are flavored with honey and spices.

Ésta sí que es Nochebuena

This Is Christmas Eve

UNITED STATES

MEXICO

CD 18:21

Mexican Folk Song

Spanish: És - ta sí que es No - che - bue - na, No - che - bue - na,
English: Christ-mas Eve is real - ly here now, real - ly here now!

no - che de co - mer bu - ñue - los.
It's a night to eat *bu - ñue - los.*

Y en mi ca - sa no los ha - cen, no los ha - cen
But in my house we can't make them, we can't make them,

por fal - ta de ha - ri - na y hue - vo.
for we have no egg or flo - ur.

CONCEPT
FORM
SKILLS
SING, PLAY

Kwanzaa is a holiday that lasts seven days. Many African American families and friends get together to share stories of their history and culture. They eat traditional foods and sing songs from their culture and other African cultures.

MAP

UNITED STATES

ERITREA

HASHEWIE

Going Round

CD 18:25

Eritrean Folk Song
Words by Hidaat Ephrem

Tigrinya: **Ha - shew - i - e** } **Shew - i - e.** { **Ha e.**
English: **Go round and round** **Go e.**

Bi-ha - de ha - bir - na } **Shew - i - e.**
All to - geth - er round

Ha-shew - ie e - na - bel - na } **Shew - i - e.**
Say - ing round and round

Leader
A - lem kit - fel - to
So the world would know } **Group** Shew - i - e.

Leader
Ku-lu - me - nin - et - na
Know___ who we are } **Group** Shew - i - e.

Leader
Ha-shew - i - e ni - bel
Let us say out loud } **Group** Shew - i - e.

Leader
Ne-fa - lit - a - di - na
This is who we are } **Group** Shew - i - e.

Go back to the beginning and sing to the End.
(Da Capo al Fine)

Leader
Bi-ha - de ha - bir - na
All to - geth - er round } **Group** Shew - i - e.

Martin Luther King, Jr., was a great American leader. He had a dream of freedom for everyone.

Martin Luther King

CD 18:29

Words and Music by Mary Donnelly
Arranged by George L.O. Strid

Mar - tin Lu-ther King.___ Mar - tin Lu-ther King.___

He had a dream_ for A - mer - i - ca.___

Mar - tin Lu - ther King.___

He was a man who want - ed jus - tice
He was a man who loved his coun - try,

more than an - y - thing._____
now his name we sing._____

He was a man who died for free - dom.
He taught us how to make a dif - 'rence.

Mar - tin   Lu - ther   King._____
Mar - tin   Lu - ther   King._____

_____ Ev' - ry - bod - y sing!   Mar - tin   Lu - ther   King!_

Mar - tin   Lu - ther   King!_   Sing,   Mar - tin   Lu - ther,

Mar - tin   Lu - ther,   Mar - tin   Lu - ther   King!

Play these patterns with the song.

Chinese people celebrate the New Year in late January or early February. It is a celebration of family and friends, gift giving, and special food.

 LISTENING CD 18:32

Dragon Dance (Chinese folk music)

The dragon means good wishes to Chinese people. During the New Year celebration, there is music in the streets. Groups of people wear big dragon costumes and move through the streets.

 Use *World Instruments* **CD-ROM** to learn more about Asian instruments.

Sing this song about the Chinese New Year.

MAP

UNITED STATES

CHINA

Bei Fang Chre

North Wind Blows

Collected and Transcribed by Kathy B. Sorensen
English Words by Linda Worsley

Mandarin: 北 风 那 个 吹　　雪 花 那 个 飘　　雪

English: The north wind_ blows,___ the north wind_ blows.___ And

花 那 个 飘　　年 来 到

snow - flakes are fly - ing, the new year has_ come.

CONCEPT
RHYTHM, MELODY

SKILLS
SING, READ

Valentine's Day is a time of fun!
What would you send your Valentine?

Skinnamarink

CD 19:5

Tin Pan Alley Song

Skin-na-ma-rink a-dink a-dink, skin-na-ma-rink a-doo,

I love you; Skin-na-ma-rink a-dink a-dink,

skin-na-ma-rink a-doo, Yes, I do.

I love you in the morn-ing and in the af-ter-noon,

I love you in the eve-ning, 'neath the sil - v'ry moon.

Skin-na-ma-rink a-dink a-dink, skin-na-ma-rink a-doo,

I love you.

You Are My Sunshine

CD 19:8

Words and Music by
Jimmie Davis and Charles Mitchell

do You are my sun - shine, __ my on - ly sun - shine. __

You make me hap - py _____ when skies are gray. __

You'll nev - er know, Dear, ___ how much I love you, __

Please don't take my sun - shine a - way. _____

George Washington fought for freedom. He became the first President of our country.

 LISTENING CD 19:11

Washington's Birthday by Charles Edward Ives

Charles Edward Ives was an American composer. He played the drums in his father's band when he was 12 years old. This music celebrates Washington's birthday.

Move your hands up when you hear this instrument.

This instrument is called a jaw harp.

Sing a song about George Washington.

Who Chopped the Cherry Tree Down?

CD 19:12

Words and Music by Ruth Norman

Solo
Hide your eyes and you will see who chopped down the

All
cher - ry tree. Who chopped the cher - ry tree down?

Solo
Who chopped the cher - ry tree down? Who did? I did!

All *Solo* *All*
Who did? I did! { He She } chopped the cher - ry tree down.

CONCEPT
FORM
SKILLS
SING, LISTEN

Purim is a day of rejoicing for the Jewish people. Children make up plays about brave Queen Esther. She saved the Jewish people a long time ago.

Ani Purim

Purim

MAP
UNITED STATES
ISRAEL

CD 19:15

Music by Nachum Nardi

Hebrew: אֲ - נִי פוּ-רִים אֲ - נִי פוּ-רִים חַ - מָ - וּם - דֶ - חַ

English: A - ni Pu-rim, A - ni Pu-rim, it comes but once a year.___

ה - לֹא רַק פֶּ-עַם בָּ - שָׁ - נָה אֲ-בוֹא לְ - הִתְ - אָ - רֵ - חַ

We all dress up and cel - e - brate, We sing and dance and cheer.___

Hoo - ray for Mor-de-chai! Hoo - ray for Es - ther!

Hoo - ray for hol - i - days! At last it's here!

372

Cherkassiya (Israeli folk dance)

Children in Israel wear costumes on Purim. How many parts does this Israeli dance have?

Listening Map for Cherkassiya

Move the same way for each A. Copy your cat leader during B.

CONCEPT
STYLE, BACKGROUND
SKILLS
LISTEN, READ

The shamrock is the symbol of Ireland. It is a tradition to wear green on St. Patrick's Day.

 LISTENING CD 19:20

St. Patrick's Day (Irish folk music)

On St. Patrick's Day, there are parades all over the country. Bands play Irish music.

Listening Map for St. Patrick's Day

Introduction

a

4 Times

a

a

b

a

b

a

This song is about an Irishman who can do many kinds of jobs.

Find Irish words in this song.

SPRING

CONCEPT
RHYTHM

SKILLS
SING, READ

Earth Day

Earth is our home. How does your neighborhood celebrate Earth Day?

Big Beautiful Planet

CD 19:24

Words and Music by Raffi

Refrain

do

There's a big beau-ti-ful plan-et in the sky,

And it's my home,_____ It's where I live.

You and man-y oth-ers live here too._____

The earth is our home,_____ It's where we live.

Verse

1. We can feel the pow-er of the noon-day sun,
2. We can feel the spir-it of a blow-ing wind,

A blaz-ing ball of fire___ up a-bove.
A might-y source of pow-er in our lives.

Shin-ing light and warmth e-nough for ev-ery-one,
Of-fer-ing an-oth-er way to fill our needs,

Sing Refrain after each verse.

A gift to ev-'ry na-tion from a star.
Na-ture's gift to help us car-ry on.

377

CONCEPT
DYNAMICS
SKILLS
LISTEN, SING

In spring the weather starts to get warmer.
It is a time of changes.

LISTENING CD 19:27

Appalachian Spring
by Aaron Copland

Aaron Copland was a famous
American composer. He composed
this music for a great dancer,
Martha Graham. It is a celebration
of spring.

Welcome Is the Month of May

CD 19:28

Words and Music by Mary Donnelly

1. See the rob - in on the wing,
2. When the hills are new - ly green,

bring - ing us a sign of spring.
all the air is fresh and clean.

Flow - ers bloom - ing ev - 'ry - where;
Bum - ble - bee and but - ter - fly

378

What signs of spring can you find in
"Welcome Is the Month of May"?

CONCEPT
RHYTHM
SKILLS
LISTEN, SING

More than 130 years ago, Mexicans won a major battle. Today they celebrate that victory with a holiday called *Cinco de Mayo*.

LISTENING CD 19:31

Sones de mariachi by Blas Galindo

Blas Galindo was a Mexican composer. He liked to use folk music to create new music.

EL PALOMO Y LA PALOMA

The Doves

CD 19:32

Mexican Folk Song
Adapted by José-Luis Orozco
English Words by Linda Worsley

Verse

Spanish: El pa - lo - mo y la pa - lo - ma se sa - lie - ron
English: Mis-ter Dove and Miss Dove, they went out one day to

a pa - sear. El pa - lo - mo le de -
fly a - round. Mis - ter Dove said, "Miss Dove,

cí - a ven - te que voy a bai - lar.
would you dance with me? Let's go on down."

Refrain

El pa - lo - mo⌣y la pa - lo - ma los dos fue - ron a bai - lar,
Both of them came fly - ing down to land and dance up - on the ground.

y⌣el pa - lo - mo le de - cí - a
Mis - ter Dove soon had to stop; he

yo ya quie - ro des - can - sar. El pa - sar.
said, "I'm just too tired to hop." Both of hop."

LOG ON

See **music.mmhschool.com** to research Mexican music.

SUMMER

CONCEPT
BEAT, METER
SKILLS
SING, READ

Seasonal Songs

Summer is a good time to grow fruits and vegetables. In the Philippines there are two seasons, rainy and dry. The rainy season is hot. It is a good time to plant.

Name the vegetables you sing about in this song.

Bahay Kubo

My Nipa Hut

CD 19:36

Filipino Folk Song
from the Tagalog Province
English Version by John Higgins

Tagalog: 1., 3. Ba - hay ku - bo ka - hit mun - ti
English: 2. My ni - pa hut may look quite small,

ang ha - la - man do - on ay sa - ri sa - ri.
but the plants in my gar - den grow big and tall.

Sing - ka - mas at ta - long, si - ga - ril - yas at ma - ni,
There are tur-nips there are pea-nuts, there are beans all in a row.

si - tao,   ba - tao   pa - ta - ni._____
So   man - y   plants   that   I   grow._____

What sights and sounds from summer
can you find in the poem?

Up in the morning early,
The sun is first to rise;
The little birds begin to sing,
The farmers rub their eyes.
The rabbits hop down roads of dew,
The newborn baby cries,
And the gray kitten runs and leaps,
Chasing white butterflies.

Away to bed with darkness
The sun is first to go;
Across the fields with heavy wings
There flaps a shiny crow;
The children put away their toys,
Their steps are dragging slow;
And in the woods the spotted fawn
Lies close beside the doe.

—Elizabeth Coatsworth

Glossary of Instruments

A

accordion a keyboard instrument. It is a hand-held organ that is played by pressing buttons while air is forced through the instrument. It is often played while standing and held by straps over the shoulders, **178 CD 21:10**

B

bagpipe a member of the woodwind family. It is played by blowing air through a tube into the bag and then pressing the bag so that the air is forced out through the pipes, **CD 21:11**

banjo a member of the string family. It is played by plucking or strumming the strings, **191 CD 21:20**

bass drum a member of the percussion family. It is a very large drum that gives a deep sound when hit, **229 CD 20:32**

bassoon a member of the woodwind family. It is played by blowing into the reed while covering holes along the body with fingers, **228 CD 20:15**

cello the second-largest member of the string family in an orchestra. It is held between the knees and played by bowing or plucking the strings, **97 CD 20:6**

clarinet a member of the woodwind family. It is played by blowing into the mouthpiece while covering holes along the body with fingers, **70 CD 20:12**

conga a Latin American percussion instrument. It is a drum that has a low-pitched sound when struck, **24 CD 21:30**

cymbals members of the percussion family. These dish-shaped instruments are often played by hitting one against another to make a clashing sound, **29 CD 20:37**

djembe a West African percussion instrument. It is a drum made from pottery or wood that is played with the hands, **CD 21:2**

double bass the largest instrument in the string family in an orchestra. It is held upright and played by bowing or plucking the strings, **97 CD 20:7**

F

flute a member of the woodwind family. It is played by blowing across a hole at one end while covering holes along the body with fingers, **228 CD 20:10**

French horn a member of the brass family. It is played by buzzing the lips into the mouthpiece while pressing keys with fingers, **72 CD 20:20**

G

güiro a Latin American percussion instrument. It is a gourd with a bumpy surface that is scraped with a stick to make a sound, **20 CD 21:33**

guitar a popular member of the string family. It is played by plucking or strumming the strings, **61 CD 21:13**

H

harp one of the oldest members of the string family. It is played by plucking or strumming the strings with fingers, **229 CD 20:8**

K

koto a long, flat, Japanese string instrument. It is played by plucking its 13 strings, **23 CD 21:53**

mandolin a member of the string family. It is similar to a guitar, but it has a different bodyshape and 8 metal strings, **CD 21:16**

maracas members of the percussion family. The pair of Latin American rattles is played by shaking when held at the handles, **20 CD 21:35**

oboe a member of the woodwind family. It is played by blowing into the reed while covering holes along the body with fingers, **127 CD 20:13**

piano a member of the percussion family. It is played by pressing the keys on the keyboard, **17 CD 20:41**

piccolo one of the smaller members of the woodwind family. It is a small flute that plays high pitches, **228 CD 20:11**

saxophone a member of the woodwind family. It is played by blowing into the mouthpiece while pushing the keys along the body with fingers, **70 CD 20:16**

shekere an African percussion instrument. It is a hollow gourd covered with a net of beads or seeds and is played by shaking, **CD 21:8**

slit drum a percussion instrument used in Africa, Asia, and the South Pacific. It is formed by hollowing a tree trunk through a slit on one side and played by hitting with sticks, **CD 21:9**

snare drum a member of the percussion family. It is played by hitting the top of the drum with drumsticks, **229 CD 20:35**

spoons a common object used as a percussion instrument. They are played by holding two together and hitting them against the body, **37 CD 21:23**

taiko drum a member of the percussion family. It is a barrel-shaped, Japanese drum that is played with sticks, or bachi, **23 CD 21:51**

tambourine a member of the percussion family. It is a small, hand-held drum that has metal disks attached loosely around the rim, and it is played by shaking or hitting it with the hand, **24 CD 20:36**

timpani members of the percussion family. They are a set of large kettle-shaped drums that are played with mallets, **229 CD 20:26**

trombone a large, low-pitched member of the brass family. It is played by buzzing the lips into the mouthpiece while moving the slide in and out, **72 CD 20:21**

trumpet the smallest, highest-pitched member of the brass family. It is played by buzzing the lips into the mouthpiece while pressing keys with fingers, **61 CD 20:18**

tuba the largest, lowest-pitched member of the brass family. It is played by buzzing the lips into the mouthpiece while pressing keys with fingers, **72 CD 20:22**

V

viola a member of the string family. It is held under the chin and played by bowing or plucking the strings, **97 CD 20:5**

violin the smallest member of the string family in an orchestra. It is held under the chin and played by bowing or plucking the strings, **70 CD 20:4**

X

xylophone a member of the percussion family. It is played by hitting the wooden bars with small wooden hammers, or mallets **30 CD 20:30**

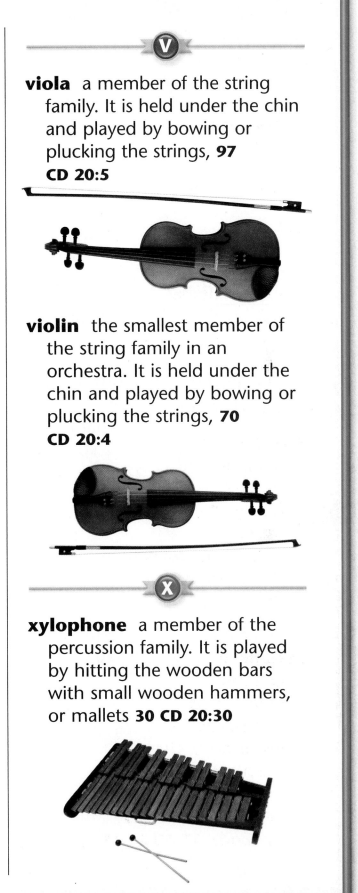

Glossary of Terms

A

accelerando gradually getting faster, **168**

aria a solo in an opera, **217**

B

ballet a story that is told through dance and music, **25**

beat a steady pulse felt in most music, **6**

brass family metal instruments such as trumpet, French horn, trombone, and tuba that are played by buzzing the lips into the mouthpiece, **228**

C

concerto music written for a solo performer and orchestra, **73**

crescendo (◁) getting louder little by little, **103**

D

D.S. al Fine Italian words that tell you to go back to the sign (𝄋) and keep going until you see the word *Fine*, **75**

decrescendo (▷) getting softer little by little, **110**

dotted half note (𝅗𝅥.) a musical note that shows a sound that is three beats long, **128**

dotted quarter note (♩.) a note equal to one quarter note plus one eighth note, **167**

downstage the area on the stage closest to the audience, **275**

dynamics the loudness or softness of music, **26**

E

eighth notes (♫) musical notes that show two sounds to a beat, **14**

F

fanfare a short piece of music to honor an important person or to announce an important event, **86**

fermata (⌢) a symbol placed over a note to show that it should be held longer than its normal value, **222**

fine an Italian word that means "the end," **75**

folk song a song that emerged from the culture of a group of people, usually of unknown authorship, **151**

forte (*f*) loud, **26**

H

half note (♩) a musical note that shows a sound that is two beats long, **87**

L

leap one way a melody moves; to move higher or lower by jumping over two or more pitches, **230**

M

melody several pitches that are sounded one after the other to make a tune, **12**

meter signature the symbol that tells how many beats are grouped in each measure, **49**

N

note a sign for a sound in music, **12**

O

opera a story told through music, **152**

P

pentatonic having five pitches, **171**, **263**

percussion family instruments such as drum, rattle, and bell that are played by striking, scraping, or shaking, **228**, **229**

piano (*p*) soft, **26**

pitch the highness or lowness of a sound, **12**

Q

quarter note (♩) a musical note that shows one sound to a beat, **14**

quarter rest (𝄽) a musical sign that shows a beat with no sound, **14**

re the pitch on step higher than *do*, **130**

rehearsing learning and practicing in order to prepare for a performance, **275**

rhythm the long and short sounds and silences that are heard in a song, **9**

ritardando gradually getting slower, **168**

rondo a musical form that has different sections, in which the A section is repeated between each different section, such as ABACA, **223**

skip one way a melody moves; to move higher or lower by jumping over a pitch, **230**

staff the five lines and four spaces on which musical notes are written, **12**

stage left the area to the left of the actor when facing the audience, **275**

stage right the area to the right of the actor when facing the audience, **275**

step one way a melody moves; to move higher or lower to the next pitch, **230**

string family instruments such as violin, viola, cello, and double bass that are sounded by plucking or by drawing a bow across strings, **228, 229**

tone color the special sound of each instrument or voice, **70**

treble clef (G clef) (𝄞) tells that the notes on the second line of a staff are called G, **18**

upstage the area on the stage farthest away from the audience, **275**

woodwind family wind instruments such as flute, clarinet, and oboe that are or once were made of wood, **228**

Acknowledgments, continued

Great Outdoors, The, from *Disneyland and Walt Disney World's COUNTRY BEAR JAMBOREE.* Words and Music by George Wilkins. © 1988. Walt Disney Music Company. All Rights Reserved. Used by Permission.

Green Eggs and Ham, From MTI's Broadway Junior Broadway for Kids SEUSSICAL Junior. Music by Stephen Flaherty. Lyrics by Lynn Ahrens. Copyright © 2001 by Warner Chappell Publishing Co., Inc., Hillsdale Music, Inc., Pen and Perseverance, Inc.

Hakuna Matata, from Walt Disney Pictures' *THE LION KING.* Music by Elton John. Lyrics by Tim Rice. © 1994. Wonderland Music Company, Inc. All Rights Reserved. Used by Permission.

Hello, Hello There, Words by Betty Comden and Adolph Green. Music by Jule Styne. Copyright © 1956 by Stratford Music Corporation. Copyright Renewed. All Rights Administered by Chappell & Co. International Copyright Secured. All Rights Reserved.

Horton Hears a Who!, From MTI's Broadway Junior Broadway for Kids SEUSSICAL Junior. Music by Stephen Flaherty. Lyrics by Lynn Ahrens. Copyright © 2001 by Warner Chappell Publishing Co., Inc., Hillsdale Music, Inc., Pen and Perseverance, Inc.

Horton Hears a Who! Two, From MTI's Broadway Junior Broadway for Kids SEUSSICAL Junior. Music by Stephen Flaherty. Lyrics by Lynn Ahrens. Copyright © 2001 by Warner Chappell Publishing Co., Inc., Hillsdale Music, Inc., Pen and Perseverance, Inc.

It's a Small World, from *"it's a small world" at Disneyland Park and Magic Kingdom.* Words and Music by Richard M. Sherman and Robert B. Sherman. Copyright © 1963. Wonderland Music Company, Inc. Copyright Renewed. All Rights Reserved. Used by Permission.

It's Possible, From MTI's Broadway Junior Broadway for Kids SEUSSICAL Junior. Music by Stephen Flaherty. Lyrics by Lynn Ahrens. Copyright © 2001 by Warner Chappell Publishing Co., Inc., Hillsdale Music, Inc., Pen and Perseverance, Inc.

Joy, from *THE FEEL OF MUSIC,* Words and Music by Hap Palmer. Copyright © by Hap-Pal Music, Inc. International Copyright Secured. All Rights Reserved.

Jugaremos en el bosque (We Will Play in the Forest), from *LIRICA INFANTIL DE MEXICO.* By Vicente T. Mendoza. Copyright © 1980 by Fondo De Cultura Economica, Av. de la Universidad 975, 03100 Mexico, D.F. International Copyright Secured. All Rights Reserved.

Let's Go Fly a Kite, from *Walt Disney's MARY POPPINS.* Words and Music by Richard M. Sherman and Robert B. Sherman. Copyright © 1963 Wonderland Music Company, Inc. Copyright Renewed. All Rights Reserved. Used by Permission.

Mama Paquita, Brazilian Carnival Song. English Version by Merrill Staton. Copyright © 1986 by Rockhaven Music. International Copyright Secured. All Rights Reserved.

Martin Luther King, Words and Music by Mary Donnelly and George L.O. Strid. Copyright © 2002 by HAL LEONARD CORPORATION. International Copyright Secured. All Rights Reserved.

Merry-Go-Round, Words by Dorothy Baruch. Arranged by Marilyn Davidson. Copyright © 1952, 1961 (Renewed 1980, 1989) by Scott Foresman & Company, International Copyright Secured. All Rights Reserved.

Oh, the Thinks You Can Think!, From MTI's Broadway Junior Broadway for Kids SEUSSICAL Junior. Music by Stephen Flaherty. Lyrics by Lynn Ahrens. Copyright © 2001 by Warner Chappell Publishing Co., Inc., Hillsdale Music, Inc., Pen and Perseverance, Inc.

On Top of Spaghetti, Words and Music by Tom Glazer. Copyright © 1963, 1965 by Songs Music Inc. Copyright Renewed. Administered in the United States and Canada by September Music Corp. International Copyright Secured. All Rights Reserved.

Orff Instruments by Donna Otto. Introduction by Janet Graham. Used by Permission.

Part of Your World, from Walt Disney's *THE LITTLE MER-MAID.* Lyrics by Howard Ashman. Music by Alan Menken. Copyright © 1988 Walt Disney Music Company and Wonderland Music Company, Inc. All Rights Reserved. Used by Permission.

Pick a Pumpkin, Words and Music by Naomi Caldwell. Copyright © 1965, 1970 (Renewed 1993, 1998) by Ginn & Company. International Copyright Secured. All Rights Reserved. Used by Permission of Silver, Burdett & Ginn, Inc.

Place in The Choir, A, Words and Music by Bill Staines. Copyright © 1978 Mineral River Music (BMI). Rights Administered by Bug Music Inc. International Copyright Secured. All Rights Reserved.

Puff the Magic Dragon, Words and Music by Lenny Lipton and Peter Yarrow. Copyright © 1963. Renewed 1991. Honalee Melodies (ASCAP) and Silver Dawn Music (ASCAP). Worldwide Rights for Honalee Melodies Administered by Cherry Lane Music Publishing Company, Inc. Worldwide Rights for Silver Dawn Music Administered by WB Music Corp. International Copyright Secured. All Rights Reserved.

Sailor, Sailor on the Sea, Words and Music by Jean Ritchie. Copyright © by Jean Ritchie/Geordie Music Publishing Co. International Copyright Secured. All Rights Reserved. Used by Permission.

Seeds and Seasons, Words and Music by Jim Walters. Copyright © Jim Walters. International Copyright Secured. All Rights Reserved.

Seussical Mega-Mix, From MTI's Broadway Junior Broadway for Kids SEUSSICAL Junior. Music by Stephen Flaherty. Lyrics by Lynn Ahrens. Copyright © 2001 by Warner Chappell Publishing Co., Inc., Hillsdale Music, Inc., Pen and Perseverance, Inc.

Sheep in the Meadow, from *Anna Banana: 101 Jump Rope Rhymes.* Compiled by Joanna Cole. William Morrow & Company, Inc. Copyright © 1989. All rights reserved. Used by Permission.

Shrimp Boats, Words and Music by Paul Mason Howard and Paul Weston. Copyright © 1951. Walt Disney Music Company, Copyright Renewed 1979. Walt Disney Music Company and Hanover Music Corporation. All Rights Reserved. Used by Permission.

Sing! Sing! Sing!, Words and Music by Branice McKenzie. Copyright © 2002 by Eunice Music. International Copyright Secured. All Rights Reserved.

Skating, Words and Music by Lynn Freeman Olson and Georgia Garlid. Copyright © 1968. (Renewed 1996). EMI MILLS MUSIC INC. All Rights Controlled by EMI MILLS MUSIC INC. (Publishing) and WARNER BROS. PUBLICATIONS U.S. INC. (Print). All Rights Reserved. Used by Permission.

Step in Time, from Walt Disney's *MARY POPPINS.* Words and Music by Richard M. Sherman and Robert B. Sherman. Copyright © 1963 Wonderland Music Company, Inc. Copyright Renewed. All Rights Reserved. Used by Permission.

Step into the Spotlight, Words and Music by Emily Crocker, John Higgins and John Jacobson. Copyright © 2004 by HAL LEONARD CORPORATION. International Copyright Secured. All Rights Reserved.

This Is Halloween, Words and Music by Teresa Jennings. Copyright © 2001 by Plank Road Publishing. International Copyright Secured. All Rights Reserved.

Acknowledgments, continued

This Is My Country, Words by Don Raye. Music by Al Jacobs. Copyright © 1940 SHAWNEE PRESS. INC. Copyright © Renewed SHAWNEE PRESS, INC. and WAROCK CORP. All Rights Reserved.

This Land Is Your Land, Words and Music by Woody Guthrie. TRO – © Copyright 1956 (Renewed), 1958 (Renewed), 1970 (Renewed) and 1972 (Renewed). Ludlow Music, Inc., New York, NY. International Copyright Secured. All Rights Reserved Including Public Performance For Profit. Used by Permission.

Tiki Tiki Room, The, from *ENCHANTED TIKI ROOM* at Disneyland Park and *TROPICAL SERENADE*. Words and Music by Richard M. Sherman and Robert B. Sherman. Copyright © 1963 Wonderland Music Company, Inc. Copyright Renewed. All Rights Reserved. Used by Permission.

Wake Up the Sun, Words and Music by John Jacobson and Emily Crocker. Copyright © 2000 by HAL LEONARD CORPORATION. International Copyright Secured. All Rights Reserved.

Welcome Is the Month Of May, Words and Music by Mary Donnelly and George L.O. Strid. Copyright © 1999 by HAL LEONARD CORPORATION. International Copyright Secured. All Rights Reserved.

What a Wonderful World, Words and Music by George David Weiss and Bob Thiele. Copyright © 1967 by Range Road Music Inc., Quartet Music, Inc. and Abilene Music, Inc. Copyright Renewed. International Copyright Secured. All Rights Reserved. Used by Permission.

Who Chopped the Cherry Tree Down?, Words and Music by Ruth Norman. Copyright © 1952 (Renewed 1980). EMI MILLS MUSIC INC. All Rights Controlled by EMI MILLS MUSIC INC. (Publishing) and WARNER BROS. PUBLICATIONS U.S. INC. (Print). All Rights Reserved. Used by Permission.

You Are My Sunshine, Words and Music by Jimmie Davis and Charles Mitchell. Copyright © 1930 by Peer International Corporation. Copyright Renewed. International Copyright Secured. All Rights Reserved.

You'll Sing a Song and I'll Sing a Song, Words and Music by Ella Jenkins. Copyright © by Ell-Bern Publishing Company. International Copyright Secured. All Rights Reserved.

You've Got a Friend in Me, from Walt Disney's *TOY STORY*. Music and Lyrics by Randy Newman. Copyright © 1995. Walt Disney Music Company. All Rights Reserved. Used by Permission.

Literature

Bliss by Eleanor Farjeon, from *Eleanor Farjeon's Poems for Children*. Copyright © 1938, 1951. Reprinted in *The Random House Book of Poetry For Children*. Selected and introduced by Jack Prelutsky. Copyright © 1983 by Random House, Inc. All Rights Reserved.

City Traffic by Betsy Franco, from *Thematic Poetry: Transportation,* by Betsy Franco & Friends. Copyright © 2001. Scholastic Professional Books.

Coyote and the Bluebirds (originally titled 'How the Bluebird Got its Color') by Katharine Berry Judson, from *Myths and Legends of California and the Old Southwest*. Copyright © 1912 by A.C. McClurg & Co, Chicago. All Rights Reserved.

Drumming Spider, The, compiled by Helen East, from *The Singing Sack: 28 Song-Stories from Around the World*. Copyright © 1989 Helen East. Published by A & C Black, Ltd., 35 Bedford Row, London WCIR 4JH. All Rights Reserved.

Elephant Carries a Great Big Trunk, The, anonymous, reprinted in *Read-Aloud Rhymes for the Very Young,* selected by Jack Prelutsky. Copyright © 1986 by Alfred A. Knopf, Inc. All Rights Reserved.

Finis by Sir Henry Newbolt, from *Goodchild's Garland*. Elkin Matthews, London. Used by permission. Reprinted in *The Arbuthnot Anthology of Children's Literature,* compiled by May Hill Arbuthnot. Copyright © 1961 by Scott, Foresman, and Company.

Hairy Dog, The, by Herbert Asquith, from *Pillicock Hill*. Used by permission of the Macmillan Company and of William Heinemann, Ltd. Reprinted in *The Arbuthnot Anthology of Children's Literature,* compiled by May Hill Arbuthnot. Copyright © 1961 by Scott, Foresman, and Company.

Happy Thought by Robert Louis Stevenson, from *A Child's Garden of Verses*. Copyright © 1905, by CHARLES SCRIBNER'S SONS. All Rights Reserved. Reset March 1955. Used by Permission.

I Heard a Bird Sing by Oliver Herford. Reprinted by permission of Helen B. Herford. Reprinted in *Piping Down the Valleys Wild*. Edited by Nancy Larrick. Published by Delacorte Press. Copyright © 1968, 1985. All Rights Reserved.

Little Seeds by Else Holmelund Minarik, from *The Winds That Come From Far Away and Other Poems*. Copyright © 1964. Reprinted in *Read-Aloud Rhymes for the Very Young,* selected by Jack Prelutsky. Copyright © 1986 by Alfred A. Knopf, Inc. All Rights Reserved.

Moon Boat by Charlotte Pomerantz, from *All Asleep*. Copyright © 1984 by permission of Greenwillow Books, a division of William Morrow & Company, Inc. Reprinted in *Read-Aloud Rhymes for the Very Young,* selected by Jack Prelutsky. Copyright © 1986 by Alfred A. Knopf, Inc. All Rights Reserved.

Opposite of Two, The by Richard Wilbur from *Opposites*. Copyright © 1973 by Richard Wilbur. Reprinted by permission of Harcourt Brace Jovanovich, Inc. Reprinted in *The Random House Book of Poetry For Children,* selected and introduced by Jack Prelutsky. Copyright © 1983 by Random House, Inc. All Rights Reserved.

Piggy by William Cole, from *Poem Stew*. HarperTrophy, a Division of HarperCollins Publishers. Copyright © 1981 by William Cole. All Rights Reserved. Used by Permission.

Señor Coyote by Pleasant DeSpain/Kirk Lyttle, from *Twenty-Two Splendid Tales to Tell From Around the World, Volume Two*. Copyright © 1979, 1990, 1994 by Pleasant DeSpain. Published by August House, Inc., P.O. Box 3223, Little Rock, Arkansas 72203. All Rights Reserved.

Sun Is First to Rise, The, by Elizabeth Coatsworth, from *Summer Green*. Reprinted in *Story and Verse for Children*. Selected and edited by Miriam Blanton Huber, Ph.D. The Macmillan Company, New York. Copyright © 1955. All Rights Reserved. Used by Permission.

Together by Paul Engle, from *Embrace: Selected Love Poems*. Copyright © 1969. Reprinted in *The Random House Book of Poetry For Children*. Selected and introduced by Jack Prelutsky. Copyright © 1983 by Random House, Inc. All Rights Reserved.

Who Has Seen the Wind? by Christina Georgina Rossetti, from *Sing-Song, A Nursery Rhyme Book for Children*. The Macmillan Company. Copyright © 1924, 1968. All Rights Reserved. Used by Permission.

Classified Index

Alphabetical Index

INDEX OF SONGS AND SPEECH PIECES

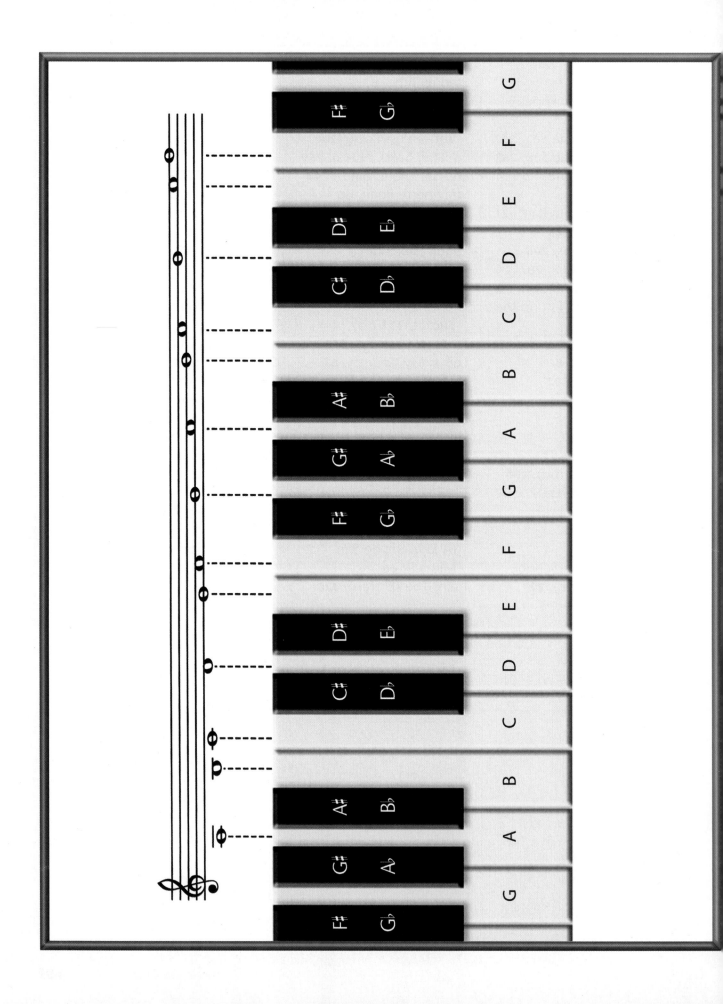

When she arrived at the stream, Spider and his family began to play the drums. The girl felt a magic rhythm in her heart. She began to dance and dance. She finally fell to the ground completely worn out.

Back at the party, the chief ordered a boy to go find the girl. When the boy got to the stream, Spider and his family began to play the drums. The boy felt the magic rhythm in his heart and began to dance.

This time, the villagers heard the music and came running to the stream. One by one they all felt the magic rhythm beating in their hearts and began to dance. Spider and his family came out from the bushes. The villagers begged them to stop playing, but they would not.

After a long time, the villagers fell to the ground and crawled home to bed. They had never been so tired. From then on, Spider was invited to all the village parties. And he and his family always ate as much as they wanted!

Spotlight on Celebrations

Spotlight on Celebrations

Songs of Our Country

People sing songs to show pride in their country. Sing "America" to show your pride in the United States.

CD 17:2

Music by Henry Carey
Words by Samuel F. Smith

do

My coun - try 'tis of thee, Sweet land of

lib - er - ty, Of thee I sing. Land where my

fa - thers died, Land of the Pil - grim's pride,

From ev' - ry___ moun - tain - side Let___ free - dom ring.